ANCIENT WISDOM, LIVING MISSION

ANCIENT WISDOM, LIVING MISSION

PREPARING PASTORS FOR WORD AND WORK THROUGH THE PASTORAL TRAINING MODEL

CHRISTIAN VOCATION IN CONTEXT: THE D. JAMES KENNEDY INSTITUTE OF REFORMED LEADERSHIP SERIES

MICHAEL A. MILTON

WIPF & STOCK · Eugene, Oregon

Theology should not be purely contextual . . . but it is always contextualized, applying the timeless truth of God's Word to the timely situations of God's people.

— COLEMAN M. FORD AND SHAWN J. WILHITE, *Ancient Wisdom for the Care of Souls* (2024)

There was nothing but land; not a country at all, but the material out of which countries are made.

— WILLA CATHER, *My Ántonia* (1918)

ABOUT THE SERIES
CHRISTIAN VOCATION IN CONTEXT

Wipf and Stock Publishers, in cooperation with The D. James Kennedy Institute of Reformed Leadership, presents *The Christian Vocation in Context Series.*

The *Christian Vocation in Context* series brings together theological, pastoral, and scholarly reflections on the nature of Christian calling in the contemporary world. Published in partnership with the D. James Kennedy Institute of Reformed Leadership, these volumes explore the intersection of Gospel proclamation, ecclesial life, and public witness within the complexities of the modern age.

Grounded in the historic Christian faith and shaped by the Reformed tradition, the series seeks to cultivate spiritually mature leaders who are equipped to serve Christ and His Church with intellectual rigor, pastoral wisdom, and missional clarity. Each volume addresses a particular dimension of vocation—public theology, pastoral formation, church planting, moral leadership, and cultural engagement—within the broader framework of the Great Commission and the Cultural Mandate.

Attentive both to classical theological sources and contemporary challenges, the series encourages thoughtful engagement with Scripture, tradition, and lived experience. The goal is to foster a robust Christian witness that is faithful to the Lordship of Jesus Christ and responsive to the spiritual and intellectual needs of the present generation.

Michael A. Milton, PhD, General Editor

President and Senior Fellow
The D. James Kennedy Institute of Reformed Leadership

CONTENTS

PREFACE

The book you are about to read emerged from research and peer-reviewed work undertaken as part of a Doctor of Ministry program. For over three decades, I have served in theological higher education and pastoral ministry—both in civilian parishes and as a military chaplain. Over the years, I became increasingly aware of a troubling pattern affecting the body of Christ, at least within the North American context.

Too often, newly ordained pastors enter the ministry with a sufficient grasp of theological knowledge—both of the head and heart—but without the seasoned wisdom that only practical experience can provide. As a result, many of these younger pastors, through no fault of spiritual intent, make critical and avoidable errors in parish ministry. The consequences can be devastating: congregational division, lasting wounds upon their ministerial records, and even deep familial strain.

I believe such outcomes are not inevitable. They can be prevented.

Thus, I undertook a course of study to identify the root of the problem and to propose a remedy. The pages that follow describe the nature of that inquiry, the results of the research, and the pastoral theology that supports the proposed model of formation. The fruit of this work is what I have come to call *The D. James Kennedy Institute of Reformed Leadership Pastoral Training Model.*

The essential components of this model—and the burden that gave rise to it—will, I trust, become evident as you read.

Michael A. Milton, PhD
Tryon, North Carolina
Holy Saturday 2026

Our soul waits for the Lord;

he is our help and our shield.

For our heart is glad in him,

because we trust in his holy name.

Let your steadfast love, O Lord, be upon us,

even as we hope in you.

— Psalm 33:20-22 (ESV)

INTRODUCTION

BIBLICAL FOUNDATIONS FOR EDUCATING AND TRAINING CHRISTIAN SHEPHERDS

Preparing shepherds for God's flock is neither a new idea nor an optional duty of the Church. Throughout history, from Moses to Paul's missionary journeys, the Bible consistently shows that God appoints leaders, provides them with the necessary skills, and then commissions them to train others. Consider these eight passages from the Old and New Testaments. The Bible does not teach a egalitarianism of pastoral ministry, as if roles do not apply in the People of God. To the contrary, the Word of God consistently underscores the importance of men called by God to proclaim His Word to the world.

OLD TESTAMENT

Numbers 27:16–17

> "Let the LORD, the God of the spirits of all flesh, appoint a man over the congregation who shall go out before them and come in before them, who shall lead them out and bring them in, that the congregation of the LORD may not be as sheep that have no shepherd."

Even at the close of his ministry, Moses' heart was for God's people to be led well. The prayer for a faithful shepherd becomes a principle for every generation: leadership transition must be deliberate, and the next shepherd must be prepared to guide God's flock.

Ezra 7:10

> "For Ezra had set his heart to study the Law of the LORD, and to do it and to teach his statutes and rules in Israel."

Ezra's ministry unfolds in three phases—study, obedience, and teaching. This sequence continues to serve as a timeless model for pastoral readiness: acquiring knowledge, practicing godliness, and developing the skill to instruct. This is not merely higher education nor on-the-job training. It is both. We educate, train, and plan such a program by prayerful obedience to the Lord, expecting that He will bless His Word applied.

2 Chronicles 17:7–9

> "In the third year of his reign he sent his officials... to teach in the cities of Judah; and with them the Levites and the priests. And they taught in Judah, having the Book of the Law of the LORD with them. They went about through all the cities of Judah and taught among the people."

King Jehoshaphat's reform was not solely political; it was profoundly theological. He instructed and dispatched teachers to disseminate the Word throughout all regions of the nation, exemplifying that leadership within God's kingdom necessitates a dedication to empowering others with the truth.

Proverbs 27:23

> "Know well the condition of your flocks, and give attention to your herds."

Wisdom literature emphasizes that pastoral ministry is a broad responsibility requiring wise servants of both God and the People. The passage envisions a group of educated, trained, and dedicated shepherds called to serve. The seminary—literally, a seedbed for pastors—must be led by pastor-teachers capable of shepherding other shepherds.

NEW TESTAMENT

John 20:21–23

> "Jesus said to them again, 'Peace be with you. As the Father has sent me, even so I am sending you.' And when he had said this, he breathed on them and said to them, 'Receive the Holy Spirit. If you forgive the sins of any, they are forgiven them; if you withhold forgiveness from any, it is withheld.'"

In the upper room, the risen Christ both restores and commissions His disciples, entrusting them with the Spirit's power for their mission. Peter's personal restoration (John 21:15–17) symbolizes the pastoral calling—redeemed servants sent to feed His sheep.

2 Timothy 2:2

> "...and what you have heard from me in the presence of many witnesses entrust to faithful men, who will be able to teach others also."

This passage describes the apostolic strategy for multiplying pastors. Saint Paul's command to Timothy lifts the young pastor's gaze toward future ministry opportunities, emphasizing a vital divine mandate to train others who will, in turn, train more—creating a relay race of gospel work across generations. Timothy must serve with this vision: "Enlist other men who are called to preach into a pastoral training ministry that goes on until Christ comes again."

Titus 1:5

> "This is why I left you in Crete, so that you might put what remained into order, and appoint elders in every town as I directed you."

Paul explains that he appointed Titus to stay in Crete to organize the believers and appoint church leaders in each town. The education and training of Christian shepherds is a normative function of the Church.

Ephesians 4:11–12

> "And he gave the apostles, the prophets, the evangelists, the shepherds and teachers, to equip the saints for the work of ministry, for building up the body of Christ."

Where there is a gathering of disciples of Christ, there must be, of necessity, a minister of the Gospel to shepherd the flock through Word, Sacrament, and Prayer. Education and training are not an option nor a luxury. God calls, and we, who have been called and conducted ministry, must then maximize our efforts and multiply ourselves in the lives of those whom God has called. The education and training of men for ministry is the non-negotiable mission of ministers of the Gospel. Moreover, the scene does not call for separate academies, but strong mentoring relationships at the parish level. Men are best prepared for Gospel ministry in the incubator of the local church, with supervising shepherds. This is the normative method for strengthening and sending forth the people of God for faith, life, ministry, and mission.

In both the Old and New Testaments, we understand that the preparation of shepherds of believers is not distinct or detached from the heart of God. Indeed, ministers must be a manifestation of God's love for His own. And so, we are called "to shepherd the shepherds who will shepherd the sheep," as we advocate at the DJK Institute, and this not for personal gain but so that human beings "may not be as sheep that have no shepherd" (Num. 27:17). This is the ancient wisdom that continues to inspire our ongoing mission.

Therefore, considering the mandate and mission, what measures should we undertake to best prepare Christian shepherds and evangelists *according to the Scriptures* in our time?

THE VISION OF THE PASTORAL TRAINING MODEL

The purpose of the Pastoral Training Model is not merely to produce competent ministers but to cultivate faithful shepherds who endure across a lifetime of ministry.

The Church in every age faces changing circumstances, yet her enduring need remains constant: pastors formed in sound doctrine, strengthened in personal holiness, and guided by pastoral wisdom. The health of Christ's Church is inseparable from the spiritual and vocational health of those called to shepherd His flock.

Through intentional formation, mentoring fellowship, and theological depth, the Pastoral Training Model seeks to integrate learning with lived ministry so that the servant of Christ is continually shaped by the Word of God and sustained through the ordinary means of grace. Word, Sacrament, and Prayer become not merely functions of office, but the very pattern of life through which the pastor grows in fidelity and fruitfulness.

By strengthening the shepherd, the Pastoral Training Model seeks to strengthen the Church, so that the people of God may be built up in faith, hope, and love, until the Chief Shepherd appears and His servants receive the unfading crown of glory (1 Peter 5:4 ESV).

THE PASTORAL TRAINING MODEL

The D. James Kennedy Institute of Reformed Leadership

1. **Pastoral Internship**
   Early immersion in supervised ministry practice

2. **Pastoral Residency**
   Intensive in-parish mentored training in core pastoral competencies

3. **Pastoral Fellowship**
   Specialized leadership development

4. **Pastoral Lifelong Learning**
   Ongoing pastoral and spiritual formation

5. **Keeper of Meaning**
   Legacy mentoring and intergenerational wisdom transfer

PART ONE

THE MODEL

1

MY RESEARCH AND THE PASTORAL TRAINING MODEL

This chapter consists of three parts. First, I present the foundational research and Digital Object Identifier (DOI) for my professional doctoral project, along with an abbreviated academic paper on the model. Second, I include an excerpt adapted from a grant-funded, peer-reviewed research paper on Reimagining Pastoral Education and Training. For those interested in learning more about the theological and mixed-method research that contributed to this book and to the Pastoral Training Model, I provide a link to the full thesis. Third, I offer a concise summary of the 273-page dissertation that followed the grant-funded research, along with expanded reflections on the biblical wisdom undergirding the model, a comparison with ancient rabbinic training traditions, an examination of global seminary reforms, and a concluding statement on the significance of the Pastoral Training Model.

I. THE RESEARCH AND DIGITAL OBJECT IDENTIFIER (DOI)

"Reimagining Pastoral Education and Training" is a professional doctoral project born out of my deep burden for the pastor-parish challenges that too often lead to early-career dropout. A fundamental prelude question shaped my inquiry: Is there really a declining corps of young pastors leaving the ministry, disrupting their families and congregations, and forfeiting opportunities for good when communities need their services more than ever? My research is unequivocal in its evidence-based conclusions: pastors are indeed leaving the ministry early in their careers.

As one who has invested more than three decades in both parish ministry and theological higher education, I found this evidence of a veritable pandemic of aborted vocations to be deeply personal. It prompted a visceral research question: How can theological higher education adapt to respond to this crisis of vocation? In the second chapter of the dissertation, I examined the literature on the relationship between vocational crisis and theological education. My findings confirmed that the presenting issue of clergy burnout and dropout is endemic to diverse Christian communities, especially in the West. Drawing on an abundance of corroborating research on North American clergy attrition, I employed a mixed-methods approach and concluded that a significant gap exists—not only in the literature but also in the lived experience of ordinands. Pastors have often received a mono-modal education that omits the vocationally grounded, parish-based training long practiced in the Church.

My research also revealed the possibility of an in-group bias among theological educators. This cognitive bias has perpetuated a scholastic model of theological higher education since at least the nineteenth century. In response, I posited a solution: we must reimagine—reconsider and refashion—a method of spiritual and vocational formation that produces biblically faithful and vocationally sustainable pastoral ministry. The proposed solution is an education and training model that unites the university and vocational models into what I call the Pastoral Training Model.

In the third chapter, I recorded my research into pedagogical methodologies in the Pastoral Epistles. The evidence of a Pauline commitment to multimodality led me to evaluate contemporary modalities, especially the role of technology. Chapter Four then examined theological and philosophical voices on technology and vocational formation. The cumulative data answered my opening questions: a multimodal teaching and learning model that embraces both the seminary and the indispensable place of the local church (or other ministry context) can make a positive contribution to pastoral education and training. In short, reimagining pastoral education and training leads us "back to the future" by recovering the Pastoral Training Model.

Reimagining Pastoral Education and Training: Defeating Pastoral Burnout and Dropout Through Uniting the University Model, the Apprenticeship Model, and Multi-Modal Theological Higher Education

Milton, Michael A. "Reimagining Pastoral Education and Training: A Doctoral Thesis on Precluding Pastoral Burnout and Dropout Through Recovery of Balance Between the University Model and the Apprenticeship Model of Theological Higher Education." figshare, 24 May 2022. https://doi.org/10.6084/m9.figshare.19858144.v1.

ResearchGate: https://doi.org/10.6084/m9.figshare.19858144.v1

BIBLICAL WISDOM AND THE PASTORAL TRAINING MODEL

Biblical wisdom is far more than intellectual knowledge or doctrinal precision. It is the skillful, Spirit-directed application of God's timeless truth to the complex realities of life and ministry. Scripture itself defines this wisdom as beginning with "the fear of the LORD" (Proverbs 9:10; 1:7) and flowering in practical godliness, discernment, and humble service. It is relational, experiential, and proven in the crucible of real-life obedience. As James reminds us, "Who is wise and understanding among you? Let them show it by their good life, by deeds done in the humility that comes from wisdom" (James 3:13, NIV).

Throughout the Pastoral Epistles, the Apostle Paul models this wisdom with remarkable clarity. He does not merely transmit theological information to Timothy and Titus; he mentors them in the full spectrum of pastoral life—preaching the Word, caring for souls, exercising leadership, enduring hardship, maintaining personal holiness, and raising up faithful successors (2 Timothy 2:2). Paul's approach is inherently *multimodal*: it combines formal instruction, personal example, shared ministry in the local church, and ongoing accountability. He writes, "You, however, have followed my teaching, my conduct, my aim in life, my faith, my patience, my love, my steadfastness" (2 Timothy 3:10, ESV). This is ancient biblical wisdom in action—word and work woven inseparably together.

My research revealed a troubling gap in much of contemporary theological education. While seminaries excel in scholarly formation, many ordinands graduate with strong heads and hearts but without the seasoned, practical wisdom that only guided experience can provide. This imbalance contributes directly to early-career burnout and dropout. The Pastoral Training Model (PTM) was born out of a desire to recover the biblical pattern Paul demonstrated and the Church practiced for centuries.

The PTM therefore unites rigorous academic study (the university model) with immersive, supervised apprenticeship (the vocational model) through a multimodal delivery that mirrors Scripture's own wisdom. In the Internship and Residency phases, students and new pastors move beyond classroom theory into real-world parish life under the guidance of seasoned mentors. In the Fellowship and Lifelong Learning phases, they deepen specialized expertise while remaining rooted in community accountability. Even the culminating Keeper of Meaning phase echoes Paul's later letters from prison, where the aging apostle pours out his wisdom into the next generation so that the faith "once for all delivered to the saints" continues unbroken (Jude 3).

This is the genius of biblical wisdom: it is never abstract or isolated. It is always *contextualized*—applying the unchanging Word of God to the changing circumstances of God's people. By recovering this ancient pattern, the Pastoral Training Model equips pastors not merely to survive ministry but to thrive in it, leading with courage, compassion, and joy for the glory of Christ and the good of His Church.

In short, the PTM does not innovate; it recovers. It takes the timeless wisdom of Scripture—especially the Pastoral Epistles—and applies it as a living mission for our secular age.

COMPARISON TO RABBINIC TRAINING TRADITIONS

In developing the Pastoral Training Model, I have reflected deeply on the rich heritage of religious leadership formation across the Abrahamic faiths. One particularly instructive parallel is the ancient and enduring tradition of rabbinic training in Judaism. While the theological foundations of rabbinic Judaism and Christian pastoral ministry differ profoundly—most notably in our shared commitment to the New Testament revelation of Jesus Christ as the fulfillment of the Torah—the structural and pedagogical wisdom embedded in rabbinic formation offers illuminating points of contact with the biblical pattern I recovered in the Pastoral Epistles. Far from innovation, the PTM stands in continuity with this broader ancient wisdom of holistic, mentor-driven preparation for spiritual leadership.

Rabbinic training traces its roots to the post-Second Temple era (after 70 CE), when Judaism shifted from a Temple-centered, priestly system to a text-centered, rabbinic one. In the earliest phases, aspiring rabbis (*talmidim*) entered a rigorous apprenticeship under a master teacher. This was not merely academic; it was immersive and relational. Students lived with, served, and imitated their rabbi—literally walking in his "dust," as the tradition described it—so that they absorbed not only Torah and Talmud but the very character and conduct of a faithful teacher of Israel. The process culminated in *semikhah* (ordination), originally conferred through the laying on of hands, a practice that traces back to Moses and Joshua. Over time, as the oral tradition was codified in the Mishnah and Talmud, training moved into formal academies (*bet midrash* and later yeshivas). There, students engaged in intensive textual study, dialectical debate (*pilpul*), and halakhic reasoning, all while learning to apply the law practically in community life. Lifelong learning remained central: rabbis continued to study, teach, and serve congregations long after ordination, transmitting wisdom across generations.

This model strikingly echoes the Apostle Paul's own formation and practice. Paul himself was trained in the rabbinic tradition under Gamaliel (Acts 22:3), one of the leading Pharisees of his day. When Paul mentored Timothy and Titus, he employed the same multimodal approach: formal instruction, personal example, shared ministry in the local church, supervised practice, and accountability.

The similarities between rabbinic training and the PTM are therefore substantial and instructive:

- Apprenticeship as the Heart of Formation: Both systems reject purely scholastic models in favor of guided, hands-on experience under a seasoned mentor.
- Multimodal Learning: Rabbinic education combined intensive textual mastery with practical application in community life. The PTM achieves the same balance through hybrid delivery.
- Holistic Development: Both traditions form the whole person—head, heart, and hands.
- Lifelong Transmission: Rabbinic wisdom culminates in the teacher becoming a "keeper of meaning" for the next generation, precisely as the PTM's final phase intends.

Important distinctions remain. Rabbinic training centers on halakhic mastery and the interpretation of the Torah and the Talmud, whereas the PTM is grounded in the full canon of Scripture, with a special emphasis on the gospel of grace, the Great Commission, and the shepherding heart of Christ. By recovering and adapting this ancient wisdom—biblical, apostolic, and informed by the best of historic religious formation—the Pastoral Training Model offers a biblically faithful path forward: rigorous scholarship married to relational apprenticeship, producing pastors who are not only learned but wise.

GLOBAL SEMINARY REFORMS AND THE PASTORAL TRAINING MODEL

The crisis of pastoral burnout and early-career dropout that prompted my doctoral research is not confined to North America. It is a global phenomenon. The dramatic shift of Christianity's center of gravity to the Global South—particularly across Africa, Asia, and

Latin America—has created both unprecedented opportunity and an acute leadership crisis for the Church. Explosive church growth has far outpaced the capacity of traditional residential seminaries. In many regions, estimates suggest that only about five percent of pastors have received any formal theological training, while the global need for equipped leaders is estimated at over 3.7 million. This reality has ignited widespread reform efforts in theological education worldwide.

Key developments in global seminary reform include:

- Competency-Based Theological Education (CBTE) and Theological Education by Extension (TEE): Long-established and rapidly expanding across Africa, Asia, and Latin America, these approaches move beyond classroom-centric models to emphasize demonstrated ministry competencies, character formation, and contextual application within local church settings.
- Hybrid, multimodal, and church-embedded training: Institutions and networks worldwide are blending online instruction, in-person intensives, and supervised apprenticeship to make theological education more accessible, affordable, and rooted in real ministry contexts.
- Contextualization and holistic formation: There is a strong emphasis on curricula that are biblically faithful yet deeply responsive to local cultures, languages, and challenges, while integrating spiritual discipleship, leadership development, and practical skills.
- Collaborative networks and "trainers of trainers" multiplication: Organizations such as the International Council for Evangelical Theological Education (ICETE)—which connects nearly 1,000 evangelical seminaries and training programs across more than 80 countries—have become leading catalysts for quality assurance,

innovation, and partnership in response to these global realities.

These reforms reflect a shared conviction that the nineteenth- and twentieth-century scholastic model, while valuable for academic rigor, is insufficient to meet the demands of twenty-first-century ministry in a rapidly changing, majority-world Church. The Pastoral Training Model (PTM) was developed in direct conversation with this global context. By uniting rigorous academic theology with immersive, mentor-guided apprenticeship through clearly defined phases—Internship, Residency, Fellowship, Lifelong Learning, and the culminating Keeper of Meaning—the PTM recovers the ancient biblical pattern of formation modeled by the Apostle Paul while addressing many of the very gaps that current worldwide reforms seek to close.

Where many global initiatives focus on flexibility and contextualization, the PTM adds structured, lifelong accountability and a clear pathway from initial formation to mature legacy. Its multimodal delivery and strong emphasis on local-church partnership make it scalable and adaptable across cultures. In this global moment of reformation, the PTM stands as both a participant in and a contributor to the renewal of theological education. It is my deep prayer that this model may serve as one useful instrument among many that the Lord is raising up to equip faithful shepherds for His Church in every nation, culture, and generation.

II. THE PASTORAL TRAINING MODEL: ADDRESSING BURNOUT THROUGH INTEGRATED MINISTERIAL FORMATION

Pastoral ministry is a noble calling, yet it is fraught with unique demands that often lead to discouragement, fatigue, and burnout. In response to these realities, I developed the Pastoral Training Model

(PTM) as President of the D. James Kennedy Institute of Reformed Leadership. The PTM offers a comprehensive solution by integrating rigorous academic and theological education with supervised pastoral apprenticeship. This approach fosters resilient, well-rounded spiritual leaders capable of navigating the complexities of modern ministry while mitigating burnout.

The PTM addresses deficiencies in traditional ministerial training by emphasizing holistic development across four phases—Internship, Residency, Fellowship, and Lifelong Learning—culminating in a fifth phase, Keeper of Meaning. This structured progression ensures the assimilation of theological knowledge, practical skills, and emotional resilience, moving beyond siloed approaches to ministerial preparation. By blending academic rigor with practical application and personal spiritual development, the PTM bridges the gap between theology and pastoral care, fostering a dynamic, responsive ministry that revitalizes both the minister and the congregation.

PASTORAL INTERNSHIP

Purpose: Introduce theological students to practical ministry through supervised experience.

Key Elements: The Internship phase immerses students in real-world ministry, guided by seasoned pastors. By combining online lectures, in-person peer-group learning, and hands-on practice, this phase ensures that theoretical knowledge is applied in practical settings. Interns engage in foundational tasks such as preaching, pastoral care, and community engagement, fostering an early integration of theology and praxis. By grounding academic study in supervised experience, the Internship phase cultivates a pastoral identity rooted in humility and service.

PASTORAL RESIDENCY

Purpose: Deepen practical competencies through intensive, mentored training post-seminary.

Key Elements: The Residency phase focuses on mastering twelve core pastoral competencies, including preaching, pastoral care, administrative leadership, conflict resolution, and personal well-being. Residents participate in weekly one-on-one mentoring, online lectures, and in-person intensives, receiving immediate feedback to integrate theoretical knowledge with practical skills. This structured support system facilitates a seamless transition from academic study to active ministry, countering the isolation and overwhelming responsibilities that contribute to burnout.

PASTORAL FELLOWSHIP (YEARS 2–4 POST-SEMINARY)

Purpose: Cultivate specialized expertise and leadership for long-term ministry effectiveness.

Key Elements: The Fellowship phase enables pastors to specialize in areas such as church planting, chaplaincy, or theological education through advanced theological study and practical application. Participants engage in doctoral-level work or focused residencies, contributing to scholarly discourse in practical theology. Mentored by experienced practitioners, fellows develop deep expertise, ensuring continuous professional growth and preventing stagnation.

PASTORAL LIFELONG LEARNING

Purpose: Ensure ongoing intellectual and spiritual growth for sustained ministerial effectiveness.

Key Elements: Lifelong Learning emphasizes continuous engagement with theological scholarship, spiritual disciplines, and peer mentorship. Pastors participate in professional development programs, integrating new insights into their practice to remain relevant and adaptable. This phase addresses emerging challenges, such as digital transformation in ministry, fostering digitally literate leadership, and mitigating professional stagnation and burnout.

KEEPER OF MEANING

Purpose: Facilitate a meaningful transition from active ministry to a legacy-focused role.

Key Elements: Drawing from George Vaillant's concept, the Keeper of Meaning phase supports ministers transitioning from active roles due to aging, disability, or vocational change. This stage, inspired by the Apostle Paul's mentorship in 2 Timothy, encourages seasoned pastors to share wisdom with younger generations, ensuring intergenerational knowledge transfer. Through structured mentorship and spiritual guidance, ministers maintain purpose and connection, enriching the ecclesiastical community and preventing existential drift.

CONCLUSION

The Pastoral Training Model is far more than an educational reform. It is a deliberate and urgent recovery of ancient biblical wisdom for a living mission in a secular age. By uniting rigorous academic theology with immersive, mentor-guided apprenticeship, the model directly confronts the modern crisis of pastoral burnout and early dropout. It forms shepherds who are not only equipped to endure the demands of ministry but to thrive in it with wisdom, resilience, and gospel-centered joy.

Structured through the progressive stages of Internship, Residency, Fellowship, Lifelong Learning, and the culminating Keeper of Meaning, the Pastoral Training Model restores the holistic pattern of formation that the Apostle Paul modeled in the Pastoral Epistles. It closes the longstanding and costly divide between seminary and sanctuary, between knowing and doing, between theory and lived obedience.

It is my deep prayer that this model will raise up a new generation of faithful pastors—true shepherds after the heart of the Good Shepherd—who will serve Christ's church with courage, compassion, and endurance. May the ancient wisdom of Scripture once again become a living mission in pulpits and parishes across the land, for the glory of God and the strengthening of His people in this generation and those yet to come.

S. D. G.

2
THE PROBLEM WITH PASTORS

"For we do not want you to be ignorant, brethren, of our trouble which came to us in Asia: that we were burdened beyond measure, above strength, so that we despaired even of life" (2 Corinthians 1:8, NKJV).

We drop in on the kind of text messages I have received from newly ordained pastors.

I made mistakes early on, partly out of my own insecurities, but also because it is simply not something we dealt with in seminary. It would have seemed pedantic to have a class on dealing with personalities in the session. But my mishandling of it turned my wife against the church and, ultimately, led to my leaving the ministry.

Why didn't you ask for help?

Where would I go?

I don't know; maybe your senior pastor...?

He was struggling with the same issues. In fact, he left the church, too.

There is a problem with pastors today. Yes, moral, ethical issues, and theological concerns need to be addressed. But if we only talk about those involved in faithful biblical and Christ-centered ministries, there is another problem—a crisis, if you prefer. The Apostle Paul's words in 2 Corinthians 1:8 reveal a truth every pastor knows well: ministry can be a crucible, testing the limits of strength and spirit. Pastors, called to shepherd God's people, often face overwhelming demands—sermons to preach, souls to counsel, communities to lead—that can lead to burnout or even leaving the ministry. My heart aches for colleagues who, like Paul, have felt "burdened beyond measure," and for congregations left wounded by such losses. This book, *Ancient Wisdom, Living Mission: Preparing Pastors for Word and Work,* proposes a better way: a **Pastoral Training Model** that combines timeless biblical truths with practical, hands-on apprenticeship to equip pastors for sustainable, faithful service.

THE PROBLEM: PASTORAL BURNOUT AND DROPOUT

In North America, three pastors leave the ministry every day, often due to burnout, unrealistic expectations, or lack of preparation for the complexities of pastoral life (Krejcir 2011). This crisis is not just personal—it affects families and congregations, leaving spiritual and organizational scars. The story of Pastor Andrew Clarke (a pseudonym), a young minister at Ephesus Presbyterian Church, illustrates this tragedy. Andy arrived eager to serve, but overwhelming demands—youth ministry, administrative tasks, and governance conflicts—led to his resignation within months. His story is not unique. Research shows that early-career pastors face role overload, conflict, and isolation, often without the tools to navigate these challenges (Elkington 2013).

WHY DOES THIS HAPPEN?

Traditional seminary education excels in teaching doctrine (the "Word") but often falls short in preparing pastors for the practical realities of ministry (the "Work"). Academic rigor is essential, but without apprenticeship in real-world settings, pastors enter churches ill-equipped for the emotional, relational, and organizational demands of their calling. This gap inspired my burden: to reimagine pastoral education by drawing on ancient wisdom—rooted in Scripture and church history—and applying it to the living mission of today's church.

A VISION: THE PASTORAL TRAINING MODEL

This book proposes the Pastoral Training Model (PTM), a four-phase program—Internship, Residency, Fellowship, and Lifelong Learning—that combines academic study with supervised ministry. Inspired by Paul's mentorship of Timothy and Titus, the PTM blends classroom instruction with hands-on practice, ensuring pastors are formed both intellectually and practically. Like medical training, which pairs medical school with residency, the PTM prepares pastors to handle the pressures of ministry while fostering resilience, community, and continual growth.

WHY ANCIENT WISDOM?

The Bible offers a timeless model for pastoral training. In the Pastoral Epistles, Paul mentors Timothy and Titus not only in doctrine but in the art of ministry—preaching, leading, and caring for God's people. This apprenticeship model, seen in the early church and historical practices, contrasts with the modern university approach, which tends to prioritize information over formation. By reclaiming this ancient wisdom, we prepare pastors for a living mission, equipping them to face today's challenges with proven practices.

WHY A LIVING MISSION?

Ministry today demands adaptability. After COVID-19, pastors face new realities—hybrid worship, digital engagement, and increased mental health needs. The PTM uses multimodal learning (lectures, peer interaction, supervised practice) to prepare pastors for these complexities. It promotes not just knowledge but character, resilience, and community, ensuring pastors thrive in their calling.

This book aims to:

1. Identify the problem: explore the causes of pastoral burnout and dropout, drawing on research and real-world stories.

2. Ground the solution in Scripture: examine the Pastoral Epistles and Jesus' ministry to establish a biblical foundation for holistic training.

3. Learn from history: trace the evolution of theological education, from apprenticeship to university models, to inform the PTM.

4. Propose a practical model: detail the PTM's four phases, designed to bridge the gap between seminary and parish.

5. Address modern challenges: consider how multimodal learning and technology can enhance vocational formation in a post-COVID, secularized Western world.

This work is for the universal church—pastors of all denominations, seminarians, professors, and lay leaders who long for a church led by shepherds equipped for both Word and Work. My prayer is that the

PTM will not only prevent burnout but also inspire a new generation of pastors to lead with courage, wisdom, and joy.

3
THE PASTOR–SCHOLAR TRADITION

"Preach the word; be ready in season and out of season; reprove, rebuke, and exhort, with complete patience and teaching."

(2 Timothy 4:2 ESV)

The Calling of the Shepherd

Pastoral ministry has never been a casual vocation. From the earliest days of the Church, the office of pastor has required the union of deep spiritual devotion, disciplined intellectual labor, and compassionate pastoral care. The minister of the Gospel is entrusted with the care of souls, and such a charge requires wisdom formed both by the Word of God and by the accumulated reflection of the Church across the centuries.

The Apostle Paul described this responsibility with unmistakable clarity when he exhorted the elders of Ephesus:

"Pay careful attention to yourselves and to all the flock, in which the

Holy Spirit has made you overseers, to care for the church of God" (Acts 20:28 ESV).

The pastor is therefore both guardian and guide—one who proclaims the truth of Christ and shepherds the people of God toward maturity in faith. This sacred task requires more than enthusiasm or sincerity. It demands learning, discernment, prayer, and perseverance.

The Church historically recognized this reality and developed traditions of pastoral formation designed to cultivate ministers who were both **faithful theologians and wise shepherds**.

The Early Church Vision

Among the earliest and most influential expressions of pastoral theology is the work of Gregory the Great. Writing in the sixth century, Gregory composed his *Pastoral Rule*, a work that became one of the most important manuals of ministry in Christian history.

Gregory famously wrote:

"The government of souls is the art of arts."

By this phrase, he meant that no task requires greater wisdom than the shepherding of human souls. Pastors must understand Scripture, doctrine, human nature, temptation, suffering, and hope. They must speak with authority while exercising humility. They must guide others toward holiness while guarding their own hearts against pride.

Gregory insisted that pastors must cultivate both **learning and character**. Without learning, the pastor cannot teach the truth. Without character, he cannot embody it.

And so, the early Church understood pastoral ministry as a calling that demanded **lifelong formation**.

The Reformation Recovery of Pastoral Learning

During the Protestant Reformation, the recovery of the Gospel was accompanied by a renewed emphasis on the training of ministers. Reformers believed that the preaching of Scripture stood at the center of the Church's life, and therefore, pastors must be thoroughly trained in theology and biblical interpretation.

Among the great teachers of the Reformation was John Calvin. Calvin believed that pastoral ministry required careful study and disciplined thought. Ministers were expected to be students of the Scriptures and interpreters of the Christian faith.

For Calvin, the pastor's responsibilities included both **teaching and shepherding**. He wrote that ministers are called to feed the flock with sound doctrine while guiding believers toward holy living.

This vision required pastors who were deeply grounded in theology. Calvin's academy in Geneva became one of the most important centers of pastoral training in Europe, preparing ministers who would carry the Reformation across the continent.

Thus, the Reformation reestablished a conviction that has remained central to Protestant ministry: **the pastor must be a theologian of the Word**.

The Puritan Pastor

This Reformation vision of pastoral ministry reached remarkable depth among the English Puritans of the seventeenth century. These ministers believed that pastoral care required not only faithful preaching but also personal engagement with the spiritual lives of their congregations.

One of the most influential voices of this movement was Richard Baxter.

Baxter served as a parish minister in Kidderminster, England, where he developed a comprehensive model of pastoral care that included preaching, catechesis, and systematic visitation of families.

In his classic work *The Reformed Pastor*, Baxter wrote:

"Take heed to yourselves, lest you be void of that saving grace of God which you offer to others."

For Baxter, pastoral ministry required careful attention both to the life of the pastor and to the spiritual well-being of the congregation. Ministers must preach faithfully, but they must also know their people personally. Baxter urged pastors to visit homes, ask about the faith of their parishioners, and guide them patiently in the Christian life.

This approach reflected a profound understanding of the pastoral calling. The shepherd must proclaim the truth publicly, but he must also apply it personally.

The Puritans developed a model of ministry in which the pastor was both a teacher and a physician of souls.

Learning and Love

Across these historical traditions—from the early Church to the Reformation and the Puritan movement—a consistent pattern emerges.

Faithful pastoral ministry requires the union of **learning and love**.

The pastor must study diligently so that he may rightly interpret the Word of God. Yet knowledge alone is not enough. The shepherd must also love the flock entrusted to his care.

The Apostle Peter described this balance when he exhorted elders:

"Shepherd the flock of God that is among you, exercising oversight, not under compulsion, but willingly, as God would have you" (1 Peter 5:2 ESV).

This union of truth and compassion defines the pastoral vocation.

The Pastor–Scholar Ideal

From these historical foundations emerges what may be called the **pastor–scholar ideal**.

The pastor is called to be a scholar—not in the sense of academic isolation, but in the sense of disciplined devotion to the truth of God's Word. The pastor must study Scripture, theology, history, and the human condition so that he may guide the people of God with wisdom.

At the same time, the pastor is called to be a shepherd who walks among the flock. He must preach, counsel, visit, comfort, and encourage. His learning must serve the spiritual welfare of the congregation.

So, the minister of the Gospel stands at the intersection of **theology and life**.

He is a servant of the Word and a shepherd of the people.

Recovering the Tradition

In many places today, pastoral ministry has been weakened by the separation of scholarship from pastoral practice. Some ministers are trained primarily as administrators or motivational speakers rather than as theologians of the Church. Others pursue academic study without cultivating the pastoral wisdom necessary to guide congregations.

The result has often been a fragmentation of the pastoral vocation.

The purpose of this manual is to recover the historic unity of the pastor–scholar tradition. By drawing upon the wisdom of the Church across the centuries, we seek to cultivate ministers who are:

- faithful interpreters of Scripture
- wise shepherds of souls
- thoughtful leaders of the Church
- servants of Christ's mission in the world

This vision forms the foundation of the **Pastoral Training Model** and the **Shepherd's Path Residency** described in the chapters that follow.

Toward Pastoral Formation

Pastoral ministry cannot be learned solely through books, nor can it be mastered through experience alone. The formation of a faithful pastor requires integrating study, mentorship, and practical ministry.

This integration stands at the heart of the training model presented in this manual.

The following chapters describe a pathway of formation designed to cultivate pastors who stand within the historic tradition of the Church while serving the needs of the present age.

Such ministers are not merely leaders or teachers.

They are **pastor–scholars**, shepherds who proclaim the Word of God and guide the people of Christ toward faithful discipleship.

4
WHY PASTORS STRUGGLE

"For he who sows to his flesh will of the flesh reap corruption, but he who sows to the Spirit will of the Spirit reap everlasting life" (Galatians 6:8, NKJV).

Tell me your story.

What part of it do you want to know?

I don't know. How about the hard part?

It's all hard.

Why?

It's easy to blame others. But it was just me.

Was it?

What do you mean?

Well, for instance, did you have practical-pastoral practice concerning the things you were learning? Did you learn to practise theological reflection after you applied, say, the systematic theology lessons in a parish setting?

What do you think?

The call to pastoral ministry is a sacred privilege, a chance to sow seeds of the Spirit in God's vineyard. Yet for too many pastors, this calling becomes a crucible, leading to exhaustion, disillusionment, or even departure from ministry. Studies show that three pastors leave their roles every day in North America, often overwhelmed by the demands of their work (Krejcir 2011). Why does this happen? And how can we prepare pastors to thrive, not just survive, in their calling? This chapter explores the challenges pastors face—burnout, unrealistic expectations, and gaps in training—and why a new approach, rooted in ancient wisdom and alive to today's mission, is urgently needed.

The Heavy Burden of Pastoral Burnout

Imagine a young pastor, fresh from seminary, stepping into a small church with a heart full of zeal. She's ready to preach the Word, counsel the hurting, and lead her flock. But soon, the weight of endless tasks—sermons, hospital visits, board meetings, and youth events—begins to crush her spirit. Add to that conflicts with church members or unmet expectations from her own heart, and she's teetering on the edge of burnout. This isn't just a hypothetical story; it's the reality for countless pastors, as research confirms (Elkington 2013).

Burnout isn't just feeling tired. It's a deep exhaustion—emotional, physical, and spiritual—that makes pastors feel ineffective, detached, or even cynical about their calling. Studies describe it as a "prolonged response to chronic emotional and interpersonal stressors" (Maslach et al. 2001). For pastors, these stressors come from many sources:

- **Overwhelming Workloads**: Pastors often juggle preaching, counseling, administration, and community outreach, with little time for rest.

- **Role Overload**: Many are expected to be everything—teacher, counselor, manager, visionary—without clear boundaries.

- **Conflict and Isolation**: Disagreements with church members or lack of support can leave pastors feeling alone.

I've seen this in the eyes of colleagues, heard it in their weary voices, and felt it in my own ministry at times. Like the Apostle Paul, who faced "trouble which came to us in Asia" (2 Corinthians 1:8), pastors today need more than doctrinal knowledge to endure. They need training that prepares them for the real work of ministry.

The Gap in Pastoral Training

Why are so many pastors unprepared for these challenges? The answer lies partly in how we train them. Traditional seminary education excels at teaching theology—the "Word" of our calling. Students master Greek, Hebrew, and systematic theology, but they often graduate with little practice in the "Work" of ministry—handling conflict, building resilience, or leading a congregation through change. As one scholar notes, seminaries often focus on "informational learning" (academic knowledge) but neglect "formational learning" (character and practical skills) (Naidoo 2019).

This gap isn't new. Even in the early church, Paul didn't just teach Timothy and Titus doctrine; he mentored them in the art of ministry

—preaching, leading, and caring for God's people (1 Timothy 3:14–15). Yet today's seminary model, rooted in the university system, can feel disconnected from the parish. Pastors need more than lectures; they need apprenticeship, community, and tools to navigate the storms of ministry.

A Better Way: Learning from Word and Work

Recent studies offer hope. Researchers have found that multimodal learning—combining lectures, hands-on practice, peer interaction, and self-reflection—can better equip professionals like doctors and counselors for their roles (Gilakjani et al. 2011). Why not pastors? By blending classroom learning with real-world ministry under a mentor's guidance, we can prepare pastors to face challenges with resilience and wisdom. This approach echoes the ancient wisdom of Paul's mentorship and points to a living mission for today's church.

In the chapters ahead, we'll explore how the Pastoral Training Model builds on this research, offering a practical, biblical plan to train pastors who are ready for both Word and Work. But first, let's understand the stakes: a church led by thriving pastors is a church that shines Christ's light to a hurting world.

5
THE BIBLICAL CALL TO TRAIN PASTORS

"And the things that you have heard from me among many witnesses, commit these to faithful men who will be able to teach others also" (2 Timothy 2:2, NKJV).

Why is everything so hard in ministry?

Well, ministry is hard.

I know that. But I mean it is hard to be a pastor in today's world.

I agree. Then, again, the nature of the work is such that even St. Paul had tremendous resistance and troubles. Ever hear of "Corinth?"

Yeah, I understand. But I guess I mean it's hard because ...

...Because no one ever showed you how ministry is done?

Paul's words to Timothy are a blueprint for ministry that endures—a call to pass on not just knowledge but a way of life, from one faithful shepherd to the next. This chapter turns to Scripture to uncover the ancient wisdom of pastoral training, rooted in Paul's mentorship of Timothy and Titus and in Jesus' example with His disciples. In a world where pastors face burnout and overwhelming demands, the Bible offers a model for preparing shepherds who are ready for both the Word they preach and the Work they live.

Mentorship: The Heart of Biblical Training

Picture a young pastor, Bible in hand, standing at the edge of his first parish. He's studied theology, but the real test begins: a grieving widow needs comfort, a board meeting turns tense, a sermon falls flat. Where does he turn? Scripture points to an ancient answer: mentorship. In 2 Timothy 2:2, Paul instructs Timothy to entrust what he's learned to "faithful men" who will teach others. This isn't just about doctrine; it's about shaping character, honing skills, and walking alongside a mentor who's been in the trenches.

Paul didn't lecture Timothy from a distant podium. He lived with him, traveled with him, and showed him how to preach, lead, and endure (Acts 16:1–5). This was an apprenticeship, not just education —a hands-on training that prepared Timothy for the joys and struggles of ministry. I've seen this in my own life, when a seasoned pastor took me under his wing, not just to teach me theology but to show me how to pray with a hurting family or navigate a church conflict. This biblical model, scholars note, emphasizes formation over mere information (Fee 1995).

JESUS: THE MASTER SHEPHERD AND TEACHER

If Paul's mentorship is a blueprint, Jesus' ministry is the foundation. In John 21:15–17, Jesus charges Peter to "feed My sheep," a call that blends love for Christ with care for His people. Jesus didn't just teach His disciples theology; He walked with them, ate with them, and showed them how to serve—washing feet, healing the sick, proclaiming the kingdom (John 13:14–15). His training was holistic, preparing them for both the Word (preaching the Gospel) and the Work (serving a broken world).

Today's pastors need this same balance. Seminaries teach the Word well, but the Work—counseling, leading, enduring—requires practice under a mentor's guidance. The Pastoral Training Model (PTM) we'll explore later builds on this biblical wisdom, pairing academic study with real-world apprenticeship to equip pastors for the long haul.

WHY SCRIPTURE MATTERS FOR TODAY'S PASTORS

The challenges of modern ministry—post-COVID worship, digital demands, mental health crises—might seem new, but Scripture's wisdom is timeless. Paul told Timothy to "endure hardship" (2 Timothy 2:3), knowing ministry would test his resilience. Jesus prepared His disciples for rejection and suffering, yet also for joy in serving God's kingdom (John 16:33). By returning to these biblical roots, we can train pastors who are not just scholars but shepherds, ready to lead with courage and compassion.

This chapter will explore how the Pastoral Epistles and Jesus' ministry offer a model for holistic training, one that bridges the gap between classroom and congregation. For every pastor feeling the weight of their calling, and for every believer who longs for a thriving church, Scripture lights the way forward.

6
LESSONS FROM THE PAST

"This is a faithful saying: If a man desires the position of a bishop, he desires a good work. A bishop then must be blameless, the husband of one wife, temperate, sober-minded, of good behavior, hospitable, able to teach" (1 Timothy 3:1–2, NKJV).

I miss good theological discussions with classmates.

Yeah, that is an excellent part of seminary life. But what does it bring to you now?

Does it have to bring anything? You are too utilitarian. Lighten up a bit, huh?

Well, I would, but you keep talking about how hard ministry is, and you've made some mistakes. I thought you would want to talk about it.

Wait! What mistakes? Telling off the Sunday School Superintendent for approving a curriculum that is one hair away from heresy? You mean that?

Well, did talking theology with your friends help? I mean, yeah, chatting about St. Anselm or debating supralapsarianism is interesting, but there also needs to be a mentor to help you apply that theology—applied theology. Makes sense?

Did you really say, "Neat?" I've only heard that in 1960s and 70s sitcoms.

So, you are actually watching quality TV. Good. Okay. "Cool," then. Does that make you happy?

No. But I wish I had a mentor in a parish setting, like you said.

Neat!

Don't test me, man.

Paul's charge to Timothy sets a high bar for pastors—not just to know the Word, but to live it with character and skill. This chapter looks back at the church's history, from the early apostles to the modern seminary, to uncover how pastors were trained for this "good work." Their stories, like ancient hymns, carry wisdom for today's church, showing us how to prepare shepherds who can endure the demands of ministry with grace and strength.

THE EARLY CHURCH: MENTORSHIP IN THE DUST OF THE APOSTLES

Imagine a young believer in the early church, sitting at the feet of a seasoned elder in a candlelit room. There's no seminary, no textbook—just the Scriptures, shared stories, and the daily grind of ministry. In the first centuries, pastors like Timothy learned through apprenticeship, shadowing leaders like Paul who taught them to preach, pray, and persevere (Acts 20:28). Augustine, a giant of the early church, didn't just study theology; he lived it, mentored by Bishop

Ambrose, who showed him how to shepherd souls through preaching and care (Farley 1988).

This wasn't a classroom exercise. It was life-on-life training, where character was forged alongside doctrine. I recall a moment in my own ministry when an older pastor taught me to listen—not just to a parishioner's words, but to their heart. That's the kind of formation the early church prized, preparing pastors for both the Word they proclaimed and the Work they lived.

THE REFORMATION: RECLAIMING THE SHEPHERD'S CALL

Fast forward to the Reformation, where men like John Calvin sought to restore the church to its biblical roots. Calvin didn't just write theology; he trained pastors in Geneva, blending rigorous study of Scripture with practical ministry in local parishes. His "Company of Pastors" was a community where young ministers learned to preach, counsel, and lead under the guidance of seasoned shepherds (McKee 2001). This balance of head and heart, classroom and congregation, echoes Paul's call for pastors to be "able to teach" yet "hospitable" (1 Timothy 3:2).

The Reformation reminds us that training pastors isn't just about knowledge—it's about forming men and women who embody the Gospel. Calvin's model wasn't perfect, but it showed that doctrine and practice must walk hand in hand, a lesson we need today.

THE MODERN SEMINARY: STRENGTHS AND GAPS

Today's seminaries, rooted in the university model, excel at teaching theology. Students learn Greek, Hebrew, and church history, preparing them to preach the Word clearly. But something is often missing. As one scholar notes, modern seminaries can focus more on "information over formation," leaving graduates unready for the

Work—handling conflict, leading teams, or caring for their own souls (Kelsey 1993). I've seen young pastors, fresh out of seminary, stumble not because they lacked doctrine but because they hadn't practiced the art of ministry.

The history of pastoral training, from Paul to Calvin to today, shows a timeless truth: pastors need both the Word and the Work. The Pastoral Training Model (PTM) builds on this ancient wisdom, providing a way to prepare shepherds for today's living mission—a church that reflects Christ's light in a weary world.

7
A NEW MODEL FOR PASTORAL TRAINING

"Be diligent to present yourself approved to God, a worker who does not need to be ashamed, rightly dividing the word of truth" (2 Timothy 2:15, NKJV).

Seminary was great. And, "Yes, seminary was lacking in some ways."

I know it wa great. My time was, too. I loved it. But I also had a mentor, I had theological and pastoral reflection on every part of the coursework. Afterwards, I was ordained an evangelist and had fairly close monitoering as I came into ministry. I mean "THAT" is the issue.

You lost me.

I mean, as Christian shepherds, we need ongoing mentorship, training, and, especially, theological reflection—throughout our ministry.

That sounds like a huge mountain to climb.

It is. But take it one step, one stage, one phase at a time, and you can be on Mount Rushmore!

You mean, Everest—Mount Everest.

Stop changing the subject. Okay, there, too. But I am talking about a career-long ministry to ministers, "shepherding shepherds to shepherd the flock" kind of thing.

"Shepherding the shepherds?" Nice alliteration. But what does that mean? I mean, this sounds like you would need a bishop. I am not Episcopalian, but I kinda like the concept. How can I sign up for his lifelong learning program for pastors? I am lonely out here.

Glad you asked. You don't have to be Episcopalian or even Presbyterian; you just need to confess the Apostles' Creed and Nicene Creed, along with one of the historic articles of faith (such as the Thirty-nine Articles, Luther's Catechism, Westminster Confession of Faith, Heidelberg Catechism, Baptist Faith and Message, and others). The idea is that (1) Christian shepherding is challenging, (2) we urgently need strong academic training, but (3) the traditional way of training pastors is through on-the-job experience, with a plan and support from others.

That sounds like a massive undertaking. What does this thing look like?

Did I say, "I'm glad you asked?" Well, I am. Here's how.

Paul's call to Timothy is a charge to every pastor: be diligent, not just in preaching the Word, but in living the Work of ministry with skill and faithfulness. This chapter unveils the **Pastoral Training Model (PTM)**, a practical plan to prepare pastors for both the Word they proclaim and the Work they embody. Rooted in ancient wisdom and alive to today's mission, the PTM offers a path to equip shepherds who can thrive amid the demands of modern ministry.

THE PASTORAL TRAINING MODEL: A BETTER WAY

Imagine a young pastor, fresh out of seminary, stepping into a small church. He's equipped with theology but overwhelmed by the daily demands—sermons, counseling, conflicts. Too many leave the ministry, burned out or underprepared. The PTM aims to change that by blending classroom learning with hands-on apprenticeship in four stages: Internship, Residency, Fellowship, and Lifelong Learning. Inspired by Paul's mentorship of Timothy, it's similar to medical training—pairing study with practical experience to develop pastors who endure.

Internship: This stage (following a seminary curriculum or an academic program of study that is intentionally paired with parish assignments and evaluations) combines academic study (similar to a seminary curriculum) with practical ministry experience. A pastor-in-training might study theology while preaching under a mentor's guidance, learning to apply the Word in the congregation. Objective: Seminary students have a supervising pastor to help apply every course they complete in seminary. Outcome: A more holistic graduate prepared to advance to the next stage of ministry preparation and ongoing support.

Residency: For one year (seminary plus one), the pastor sharpens practical skills—preaching, counseling, leading—under a seasoned supervisor, building confidence and resilience. Objective: Clinical preparation for further ministry through the study and application of twelve essential competencies for pastoral ministry.

Fellowship: After completing internship and residency, this stage (three to five years after residency) enhances expertise in a specific area, such as preaching or pastoral care, similar to earning a specialized degree. Objective: Identify, research, and present findings on a key ministry area that requires the pastor's development. Outcome: The pastor is prepared for long-term ministry through biblical study, theological reflection, and practical application.

Lifelong Learning: Pastors continue to grow through reflection and mentorship, staying equipped for new challenges, like navigating a post-COVID church, managing transitions like chronic illness that alter ministry, or aging.

I've seen this need firsthand in my own ministry, when a mentor's guidance turned my faltering steps into steady service. Scholars agree that blending theory and practice better prepares professionals, from doctors to pastors (Knowles 1980). The PTM draws on this wisdom, rooted in Paul's example, to train shepherds who reflect Christ's light.

WHY IT MATTERS

Today's pastors face unprecedented challenges—digital worship, mental health crises, cultural shifts. The PTM equips them with both knowledge and skills, ensuring they're not just scholars but shepherds. By returning to the biblical model of mentorship, we can prepare pastors for a living mission, ready to lead with courage and joy.

8

THE D. JAMES KENNEDY INSTITUTE: TRAINING PASTORS IN THE PARISH

"You then, my son, be strong in the grace that is in Christ Jesus. And the things you have heard me say in the presence of many witnesses entrust to reliable men who will also be qualified to teach others" (2 Timothy 2:1–2, NIV).

So, you have convinced me.

That wasn't me doing any convincing.

Right. Touché.

But I am thankful. I see a Christian shepherd inside of you that needs to be prepared.

So, back to school again.

No, this is not like getting an academic degree only. This is bringing together education and training.

I am already serving at my church. I teach Sunday School and try to be available to help young guys figure out their career paths. I hate to think about just drop-kicking that ministry. I love it.

Then, stay.

Do what?

Remain where you are. But start your education and training right there with the Pastoral Training Model.

What is that?

I am ...

Wait, I know: You are glad I asked.

Yep.

You're very predictable, you know.

I prefer to call it consistent.

Paul's charge to Timothy echoes across centuries, calling men to shepherd God's flock with grace and truth. In the D. James Kennedy Institute of Reformed Leadership, this ancient wisdom finds fresh expression, training men for pastoral ministry not in isolation but in the living context of the parish. Rooted in the biblical order of creation (1 Timothy 2:13–14), where God appointed man to lead, the Institute's Pastoral Training Model (PTM) equips newly ordained men to serve as faithful pastors. This chapter explores the PTM's four stages—Internship, Residency, Fellowship, and Pastoral Life Learning—designed to form men who lead with humility, teach sound doctrine, and shepherd their congregations in any denominational context, all while honoring the scriptural roles of men and women in the church.

A PARISH-BASED VISION FOR PASTORAL TRAINING

Picture a newly ordained pastor, fresh from seminary, stepping into a small congregation. His heart burns to preach, counsel, and lead, yet the weight of these tasks looms large. The D. James Kennedy Institute meets him in the parish, blending online theological education with hands-on ministry under a seasoned mentor. This model, inspired by Paul's mentorship of Timothy (2 Timothy 2:1–2), ensures that pastoral formation is practical, relational, and rooted in the church. Avmentor's guidance once turned my own faltering steps into confident ministry; so too does the PTM guide men to embody both Word and Work.

The PTM reflects the biblical principle of male leadership in the church, as Paul teaches in 1 Timothy 2:11–15. Women, gifted by God for vital ministries (1 Corinthians 12:7–11), are called to roles that honor the created order, learning in quietness and submission and refraining from teaching or exercising authority over men. The PTM thus focuses on equipping men for ordained leadership, while encouraging women to serve in indispensable roles, such as teaching other women (Titus 2:3–4), fostering the church's health.

INTERNSHIP: LAYING THE FOUNDATION

The Internship phase, akin to an MDiv, combines online courses—Scripture, theology, church history—with practical ministry in the pastor's own congregation. Under a mentor's oversight, a young pastor might study the doctrine of grace while preaching to his flock, grounding theology in real-life service. This phase aligns with the *Pastoral Lifecycle*'s "Preparing" stage (Galatians 1:17–18), where Paul yielded to God's call through humble apprenticeship. For newly ordained men, the Internship builds doctrinal depth and pastoral skill, preparing them to lead with confidence in any denomination.

RESIDENCY: GROWING IN COMPETENCE

The Residency phase, a one-year intensive, equips pastors with 12 essential competencies through video sessions led by Senior Fellows like Dr. George Grant, Dr. Harry L. Reeder III, and yours truly (*Pastoral Residency Syllabus*, pages 2–4). These competencies include preaching, counseling, visiting, praying, administering the sacraments, and balancing spirituality with family life. Monthly meetings with a supervisor ensure these skills are applied in the parish—delivering sermons, visiting the sick, and leading worship. Pastors complete reflection papers (30%), participate in discussions (20%), and craft a final pastoral plan (50%), integrating theology with practice (*Pastoral Residency Syllabus*, page 5).

This phase reflects the *Pastoral Lifecycle*'s "Growing" stage (Acts 13:13), where pastors labor faithfully in the fields of ministry. For a newly ordained man, Residency offers a structured path to hone skills under mentorship, ensuring he leads with biblical authority. The program's flexibility—online learning paired with parish practice—suits busy pastors across denominations, while its Reformed foundation upholds the scriptural order of male leadership (1 Timothy 2:12–13).

FELLOWSHIP: DEEPENING EXPERTISE

The Fellowship phase, a three-year program, allows pastors to specialize in areas like preaching or church planting, akin to a DMin, while remaining in their parish under supervision. Pastors reflect on their growth, identifying strengths and areas for improvement. This phase corresponds to the *Pastoral Lifecycle*'s "Mentoring" stage (2 Timothy 2:1–2), where seasoned shepherds equip others. For newly ordained men, Fellowship fosters advanced leadership, enabling them to mentor future pastors while upholding their God-given role.

PASTORAL LIFE LEARNING: A LIFELONG JOURNEY

The Pastoral Life Learning phase invites pastors to map their spiritual and vocational journey using the *Pastoral Lifecycle*'s stages—Conversion, Preparing, Growing, Mentoring, Reflecting (*Pastoral Lifecycle*, pages 2–6). Drawing on Paul's reflection ("I have fought the good fight," 2 Timothy 4:7–8), pastors anticipate challenges like burnout or transitions, growing in wisdom through mentorship and theological reflection. This phase, inspired by *A Theology of Learning*'s vision of learning as worship (pages 33–37), equips men to lead with resilience, honoring their calling as shepherds.

UPHOLDING BIBLICAL ROLES

The PTM's parish-based model reflects the biblical order of creation (1 Timothy 2:13), in which God appointed man to lead and woman to serve as a helper. As Paul warns against women teaching or exercising authority over men (1 Timothy 2:12), the PTM focuses on forming men for ordained leadership, ensuring they teach sound doctrine and govern the church with humility. Women, called to vital roles, contribute through good deeds, teaching other women, and managing households (1 Timothy 2:10, 5:14; Titus 2:3–5), complementing the church's mission. This balance guards against the false teachings Paul addressed in Ephesus, which disrupted God's design (1 Timothy 2:14).

WHY IT MATTERS

The D. James Kennedy Institute's PTM offers a biblical, practical path for newly ordained men to grow in their pastoral ministry. Rooting training in the parish ensures that theology shapes real ministry, guided by mentors who embody Paul's charge to Timothy. For conservative Christian communities, this model upholds the scriptural order of male leadership while valuing women's indispensable contributions. For the church, it promises shepherds who lead with grace, teach with authority, and serve with love, fulfilling God's mission in every generation.

This is, truly, shepherding shepherds to shepherd the flock according to the Scriptures: Ancient Wisdom, Living Mission.

BIBLIOGRAPHY FOR CHAPTER 8

Center for the Study of Global Christianity. "Quick Facts about Global Christianity." Gordon-Conwell Theological Seminary, 2023. https://www.gordonconwell.edu/center-for-global-christianity/research/quick-facts/.

Ford, Coleman M., and Shawn J. Wilhite. *Ancient Wisdom for the Care of Souls: Learning the Art of Pastoral Ministry from the Church Fathers*. Wheaton, IL: Crossway, 2024.

Meinzer, Chris A. "Preliminary Enrollment Data for Fall 2025 Shows Another Year of Promising Trends." The Association of Theological Schools, 2025. https://www.ats.edu/post/Preliminary-enrollment-data-for-fall-2025-shows-another-year-of-promising-trends.

Milton, Michael A. "Reimagining Pastoral Education and Training: A Doctoral Thesis on Precluding Pastoral Burnout and Dropout Through Recovery of Balance Between the University Model and the Apprenticeship Model of Theological Higher Education." Doctoral thesis, figshare, May 24, 2022. https://doi.org/10.6084/m9.figshare.19858144.v1.

______. "Vocation and Reform in Public Administration." Master's thesis, University of North Carolina at Chapel Hill, 2016.

Safrai, S., and M. Stern, eds. *The Jewish People in the First Century: Historical Geography, Political History, Social, Cultural and Religious Life and Institutions*. Vol. 2. Compendia Rerum Iudaicarum ad Novum Testamentum. Assen: Van Gorcum; Philadelphia: Fortress, 1976.

The Association of Theological Schools in the United States and Canada. *2024–2025 Annual Data Tables*. Pittsburgh, PA: The Association of Theological Schools, 2025. https://www.ats.edu/files/galleries/2024-2025_annual_data_tables.pdf.

Vaillant, George E. *Aging Well: Surprising Guideposts to a Happier Life from the Landmark Harvard Study of Adult Development*. Boston: Little, Brown and Company, 2002.

PART TWO

RESOURCES

9
EXECUTIVE SUMMARY OF THE PASTORAL TRAINING MODEL

The **Pastoral Training Model (PTM)** of The D. James Kennedy Institute of Reformed Leadership exists to address a growing challenge within the contemporary Church: the need for sustained pastoral formation that produces spiritually grounded, vocationally faithful, and enduring ministers of the Gospel.

Many pastors enter ministry with a sincere calling and genuine theological training, yet without the supervised apprenticeship, supported formation, and lifelong development that the Church has historically provided. The consequences are increasingly visible: pastoral isolation, fatigue, discouragement, preventable failure, and congregations weakened by instability. The PTM responds to these realities by recovering proven wisdom from the Church's historic pastoral training patterns and integrating those patterns with a research-driven approach to ministry formation (2 Timothy 2:2).

Biblical and Ecclesial Foundations

Pastoral ministry is not merely a profession. It is a sacred calling, entrusted by Christ to His Church. Scripture consistently presents ministerial formation as relational and generational: truth is received, embodied, and entrusted through faithful shepherds who train others for the work of ministry (Ephesians 4:11–13).

Accordingly, the PTM is:

- **Creedal**, affirming the apostolic faith as expressed in the ecumenical creeds;
- **Confessional**, grounded in the Reformed confessions and catechisms;
- **Great Commission focused**, committed to the proclamation of the Gospel and the fulfillment of Christ's mission in the world (Matthew 28:18–20).

The Pastoral Training Model (PTM): Five Phases

The PTM is a structured framework for pastoral formation across a lifetime of ministry. It consists of five phases:

1. **Calling**
2. **Formation**
3. **Residency**
4. **Fellowship**
5. **Lifelong Learning / Keeper of Meaning**

Each phase is designed to support faithful growth, increasing maturity, and long-term endurance in Gospel ministry.

The Shepherd's Path Pastoral Residency: The Core Training Year

At the heart of the PTM is **The Shepherd's Path Pastoral Residency**, a one-year, competency-based supervised residency designed to provide pastors with structured formation in real parish contexts.

This residency is built on twelve modules, organized into four quarters, and delivered through multimodal learning:

- Video instruction from seasoned ministry leaders
- Guided reading (including a core text plus monthly selections)
- Monthly supervised ministry events
- Verbatim reflection and theological-practical integration
- Residency Team accountability
- Supervising pastor sign-off and evaluation

Residency Year Structure: Quarters and Modules

Quarter 1: Genesis (Dr. Michael A. Milton)

1. Conversion
2. Catechesis
3. Calling

Quarter 2: Adjusting (Dr. George Grant)

4. Family
5. Spirituality
6. Parish

Quarter 3: Self-Awareness ([the late] Dr. Harry Reeder)

7. Visitation (Ministry of Presence)
8. Counseling
9. Pulpit

Quarter 4: Praxis (Dr. R. J. Gore)

10. Word

11. Sacrament
12. Prayer

This structure reflects the Institute's commitment to sequential pastoral formation—from Gospel foundations, through personal and household ordering, through pastoral presence and care, and finally to the means-of-grace practices that sustain ministry over decades.

Competency-Based Formation and Evaluation

The PTM and Shepherd's Path Residency are **competency-based**, not merely time-based. This means residents are evaluated based on demonstrated readiness and faithful growth rather than on test performance alone.

Evaluation occurs on a **Pass / Continue-to-Work (Redo-to-Standard)** basis. This model reinforces:

- mastery rather than superficial completion
- humility rather than image management
- growth rather than grade anxiety
- readiness for ministry rather than credential accumulation

Monthly Formation Cycle (Overview)

Each month in the residency follows a consistent formation rhythm:

1. **Instruction**
2. Watch the monthly lecture(s) and engage assigned learning resources.
3. **Reading**
4. Complete the designated reading: the required course textbook plus one approved monthly selection from the competency bibliography.
5. **Supervision and Goal Setting**

6. Meet with the supervising pastor to establish goals for the month and prepare for ministry practice.
7. **Ministry Event and Verbatim**
8. Participate in a supervised ministry event and prepare a verbatim reflection.
9. **Residency Team Reflection**
10. Engage theological and pastoral reflection with appropriate members of the Residency Team (supervising pastor, peer, and trusted laity/family input where appropriate).
11. **Assessment and Sign-Off**
12. The supervising pastor provides evaluation and sign-off for Pass or Continue-to-Work status.

Intended Audience and Institutional Use

The PTM serves:

- **Local churches** seeking healthy, faithful shepherds
- **Denominations and presbyteries** strengthening ministerial formation
- **Seminaries** seeking a structured post-seminary residency pathway
- **Pastors** pursuing renewal, sharpening, and supervised growth
- **Donors and partners** supporting clergy health and Gospel mission

The PTM is designed to strengthen pastors serving rural and under-served contexts as well as churches in every region and setting.

10

VALUES
OF THE PASTORAL TRAINING MODEL

Our values at the D. James Kennedy Institute of Reformed Leadership are based on our conviction about the Word of God, God's revelation throughout the history of our Lord and Savior Jesus Christ, and His mandate for believers.

1. THE AUTHORITY OF SCRIPTURE

We affirm the inerrancy and infallibility of the Holy Scriptures of the Old and New Testaments as the only rule of faith and practice.

2. THE HISTORIC CREEDS OF CHRISTENDOM

We confess the catholic creeds of the Church—namely, the Apostles' Creed, the Nicene Creed, and the Athanasian Creed—as faithful expressions of biblical truth.

3. THE REFORMED CONFESSION

We embrace the Westminster Confession of Faith, together with the Larger and Shorter Catechisms, as a faithful summary of the doctrine taught in Holy Scripture.

4. EDUCATION AND FORMATION

We believe that education (information) must be wedded to training (formation) to prepare servants of Christ for ministry in Word and Sacrament.

5. MULTIMODAL LEARNING AND APPRENTICESHIP

We hold that both teaching and learning are best served through multimodal means, combining classroom instruction, online engagement, and hands-on apprenticeship—including internship, residency, fellowship, and lifelong learning—so that the servant of Christ may be complete, equipped for every good work (2 Tim. 3:17).

11

COMPLEMENTARY FORMATION PHASES

IN THE PASTORAL TRAINING MODEL:

The **Pastoral Training Model** recognizes that preparation for ministry does not occur in a single season but across a continuum of formation. While the **Shepherd's Path Residency** serves as the central apprenticeship, the surrounding phases ensure that theological learning is applied, pastoral identity is strengthened, and lifelong growth is sustained.

Together, these phases cultivate pastors who endure in faithful ministry through integrated formation of mind, heart, and vocation.

1. Pastoral Internship

Theologia Applicata During Seminary Formation

The **Pastoral Internship** represents the first structured expression of *theologia applicata*—the application of theological learning to real-world ministry settings. Occurring concurrently with seminary education, internship integrates academic theological study with supervised ministry experience in the local church, chaplaincy setting, or other approved ministry context.

Following the historic understanding of practical theology articulated by Wilhelm Gräb, theological knowledge is not merely theoretical but oriented toward faithful practice within the lived realities of Christian life and pastoral service.

Each seminary course concludes with an applied component in which the student enters into a covenant with a supervising pastor or ministry mentor. Through this relationship, the student demonstrates the practical implications of the theological subject being studied. For example:

- preaching courses include supervised teaching opportunities
- pastoral care courses include hospital or home visitation
- worship courses include liturgical participation
- leadership courses include observation of session or board meetings
- evangelism courses include participation in outreach contexts

The internship phase introduces the student to the rhythms of ministry life while nurturing discernment of calling and development of pastoral identity.

Internship is not yet full apprenticeship, but it establishes the essential integration of theology and practice that prepares the student for residency formation.

2. Fellowship

Early Vocational Formation (Residency + Two Years)

Following completion of the Shepherd's Path Residency, the **Fellowship phase** provides structured support during the first two years of independent pastoral leadership. This period is often marked by increased responsibility, vocational pressure, and the need for continued guidance as newly installed pastors assume primary leadership roles.

The Fellowship may be formal or informal, but typically includes:

- continued mentoring relationships
- peer cohort meetings
- guided theological reflection on ministry experience
- accountability for spiritual disciplines
- leadership coaching
- vocational encouragement
- continuing education engagement

The purpose of Fellowship is to prevent vocational isolation and to reinforce patterns of healthy ministry established during residency. Many pastors encounter their greatest vocational challenges during the early years of ministry, when expectations are high but experiential wisdom is still developing.

The Fellowship phase strengthens resilience, supports continued theological reflection, and encourages sustainable ministry practices that promote long-term pastoral flourishing.

3. Lifelong Learning

Sustained Growth in Vocation and Spiritual Maturity

The **Lifelong Learning phase** recognizes that pastoral formation continues throughout the minister's life. Faithful shepherds remain students of Scripture, theology, culture, and the human condition.

This phase encourages pastors to identify one or more areas of focused development that strengthen both personal spirituality and pastoral effectiveness. Areas of concentration may include:

- preaching and homiletics
- pastoral counseling
- spiritual formation
- biblical theology
- church revitalization
- evangelism and mission
- worship leadership
- public theology
- chaplain ministry
- leadership development

Lifelong Learning may include formal coursework, guided reading programs, writing projects, retreats, spiritual direction, or peer learning communities.

This ongoing formation reflects the apostolic exhortation:

> "Give attendance to reading, to exhortation, to doctrine... meditate upon these things; give thyself wholly to them."
>
> —1 Timothy 4:13, 15 (KJV)

Lifelong learning sustains intellectual vitality, spiritual attentiveness, and pastoral adaptability across decades of ministry.

The Integrated Vision

Together, Internship, Residency, Fellowship, Lifelong Learning, and Keeper of Meaning form a continuous pathway of pastoral formation.

The Pastoral Training Model affirms that faithful shepherds are not produced through information alone, but through sustained formation in wisdom, character, and skill under the guidance of Christ and His Church.

The aim of this integrated approach is to cultivate pastors who preach the Word faithfully, shepherd the flock compassionately, and endure in ministry fruitfully for the glory of God.

12

FREQUENTLY ASKED QUESTIONS

ABOUT THE PASTORAL TRAINING MODEL

The Pastoral Training Model is a comprehensive, research-informed formation pathway developed by the *D. James Kennedy Institute of Reformed Leadership*, with generous endowment from Lily. Rooted in your **Pastoral Lifecycle** (inspired by the Apostle Paul's journey), PTM integrates the academic depth of the university model with the hands-on cultivation of the apprenticeship model, creating a lifelong formation track for ministers.[1]

What does "Reimagining Pastoral Education and Training" mean?

This phrase refers to the Institute's grant-supported, peer-reviewed research initiative that birthed PTM. It developed a multimodal system of theological formation—combining seminary learning, supervised parish ministry, and long-term mentorship—to address pastoral burnout and dropout effectively.[2]

How is PTM structured across a minister's vocational life?

Internship (During Seminary)

• Students apply *every seminary course* in a supervised ministry context.

• Includes structured theological reflection with mentors, peers, family, and faculty.

• Spans the entire seminary curriculum.

• Offered at no additional cost to the student through seminary tuition.

Residency (First Year After Seminary)

• A structured 12-month program during a pastor's first full-time appointment.

• Focuses on 12 pastoral competencies through a hybrid delivery: asynchronous lectures, supervised ministry engagement, and reflective verbatim practices.

• Intensive pastoral-theological mentorship.

• Cost: 12 post-graduate credit hours at $510/credit, plus $50 registration and $150 technical service fee.

◦ Total: **$6,320**, ideally covered by the sponsoring church or judicatory.

Fellowship (Five Years After Seminary)

• Ministers may enroll in advanced programs (e.g., DMin or ThD) focused on vocational renewal, theological deepening, and scholarly contribution.

• PTM provides guidance and formation support at no additional cost beyond degree tuition.

Lifelong Learning

• Offers ongoing seminars, courses, and resources tailored to midand later-career pastoral challenges.

• Delivered multimodally; cost varies by offering, with many available at no charge by the Institute.

Keeper of Meaning (Later-Career Phase)

Inspired by George E. Vaillant's post-generativity stage in Erikson's model, Vaillant describes the *Keeper of the Meaning* as one who preserves cultural wisdom and fosters institutional memory.[3] In pastoral terms, this is the season when ministers mentor, reflect, and guide both younger pastors and congregations through vocational transitions—retirement, disability, change of role, or academic appointment. PTM equips both pastors and churches to honor these seasons as mature continuations of pastoral calling.

Who leads and teaches in PTM?

Delivery is handled by experienced seminary faculty, seasoned practitioners, and pastoral mentors who shepherd formation across all phases.

Is PTM accredited?

While PTM itself is a formation model, the Internship and Fellowship phases may align with degree-granting institutions. Transfer of Residency credits depends on the receiving institution's policies.

Who is eligible to participate?

• Seminary students preparing for pastoral ministry.

• Recently ordained pastors in their first parish role.

• Mid-career ministers seeking renewal and scholarly engagement.

• Seasoned pastors entering the *Keeper of Meaning* phase and seeking guided transition.

What is the ultimate vision of PTM?

To form ministers who are theologically rooted, pastorally competent, spiritually resilient, and prepared for a lifetime of service—including the graceful transition to seasons of reflective and legacy-oriented ministry.

13
PASTORAL INTERNSHIP
THEOLOGIA ET PRAXIS IN SEMINARY FORMATION

Pastoral Internship establishes the foundation for ministerial identity through the integration of theological study and supervised ministry experience. The student begins to apply doctrine to lived ministry contexts under the guidance of experienced shepherds.

"Be doers of the word, and not hearers only."

—James 1:22

Internship cultivates the early formation of pastoral wisdom through applied theology within the life of the Church.

The first phase of the Pastoral Training Model is the **Pastoral Internship**, which integrates theological study with supervised ministry practice during seminary education. The Church has historically recognized that preparation for ministry requires both doctrinal understanding and experiential formation. Theology must not remain abstract; it must become lived wisdom in service to Christ and His Church.

Wilhelm Gräb described practical theology (*theologia applicata*) as the application of Christian doctrine to real-life situations and contemporary contexts. The Pastoral Training Model applies this insight by ensuring that each area of theological study includes a corresponding ministry practice.

Thus, theological education is paired with structured ministry engagement under the supervision of an experienced pastor, chaplain, or ministry leader.

Internship allows the student to begin cultivating pastoral identity through guided exposure to the responsibilities of ministry, including:

- observing pastoral leadership
- assisting in teaching ministries
- participating in worship leadership
- accompanying pastors in visitation
- engaging in evangelism initiatives
- attending leadership meetings
- participating in prayer gatherings

Each seminary course includes an applied component in which the student covenants with a supervising pastor or ministry mentor to demonstrate practical understanding of the subject matter.

Examples include:

Academic Course

Applied Component (Praxis)

1. Systematic Theology
    - Teaching a doctrinal class
2. Homiletics
    - Preaching a supervised sermon
3. Pastoral Care
    - Hospital or home visitation
4. Worship
    - Participation in liturgical leadership
5. Church History
    - Teaching a historical overview class
6. Evangelism
    - Participation in an outreach initiative

The Internship phase fosters early discernment of calling and introduces the student to the rhythms of ministry life.

The internship component of the PTM prepares the student for the more intensive formation of the Residency by establishing the essential unity between theological reflection and pastoral practice.

14
THE SHEPHERD'S PATH PASTORAL RESIDENCY
THE CENTERPIECE OF THE PASTORAL TRAINING MODEL

The Shepherd's Path Residency represents the primary apprenticeship experience within the Pastoral Training Model. Through mentored ministry, theological reflection, and competency-based formation, the resident develops the habits of faithful pastoral leadership grounded in Word, Sacrament, and Prayer.

"Feed my sheep."

—John 21:17

The residency integrates theology and practice so that pastors may serve Christ's Church with clarity, courage, humility, and perseverance.

The **Shepherd's Path Pastoral Residency** is the central formation experience within the **Pastoral Training Model (PTM)**—a comprehensive framework designed to cultivate the spiritual, theological, personal, and vocational health of Christian ministers across the lifespan of their calling.

The Pastoral Training Model arises from a historic conviction shared throughout the Church's centuries: those entrusted with the care of souls must themselves be carefully formed through theological learning, supervised ministry, spiritual maturation, and lifelong mentorship. From the early pastoral theology of Gregory the Great, to the reforming vision of Martin Bucer and John Calvin, to the experiential wisdom of Richard Baxter and the Puritan tradition, Christian leaders have understood that faithful shepherds are not merely credentialed—they are formed through disciplined study, guided practice, and sustained spiritual growth.

The Shepherd's Path Residency represents a contemporary recovery of this historic pattern of pastoral formation.

The Residency as the Centerpiece of the PTM Ecosystem

The Pastoral Training Model consists of five integrated phases designed to accompany the minister of the Gospel from initial preparation through mature ministry and mentoring leadership:

1 Internship (Theologia Applicata)

Seminary-based formation incorporating applied theology within supervised ministry contexts.

2 Residency (The Shepherd's Path)

A structured and mentored apprenticeship in pastoral ministry within the local church or ministry setting.

3 Fellowship (Early Vocational Support)

Continued mentoring and guided reflection during the early years of independent pastoral leadership.

4 Lifelong Learning (Continuing Formation)

Ongoing theological, spiritual, and vocational development throughout the pastor's ministry.

5 Keeper of Meaning (Mentor Phase)

Senior pastors invest in the next generation through intentional mentoring and leadership formation.

Among these five phases, the Residency serves as the primary bridge between theological education and sustained pastoral vocation. It provides an intentional season of guided ministry practice under the supervision of an experienced pastor-mentor.

Purpose of the Residency

The Shepherd's Path Residency exists to prepare pastors who:

- proclaim the Word of God faithfully
- administer the Sacraments reverently
- cultivate lives of prayer and spiritual discipline
- shepherd congregations with wisdom and compassion
- sustain healthy family and personal life
- endure in ministry with resilience and hope

The residency recognizes that pastoral ministry requires more than academic preparation alone. Faithful ministry emerges through the integration of theological understanding, spiritual formation, personal maturity, and practical skill.

The resident therefore learns not only what to believe, but how to live and serve as a shepherd of Christ's flock.

Competency-Based Formation

The Shepherd's Path Residency is structured around twelve pastoral competencies that reflect the historic work of the Christian shepherd:

1 Conversion

2 Catechesis

3 Calling

4 Family

5 Spirituality

6 Parish

7 Visitation (Ministry of Presence)

8 Counseling

9 Pulpit

10 Word

11 Sacrament

12 Prayer

Each competency integrates theological reflection with practical ministry experience. Residents engage in preaching, teaching, pastoral visitation, leadership participation, spiritual disciplines, and guided theological study.

Through mentored experience and structured reflection, the resident develops habits that support long-term ministry health and faithfulness.

The Pastor-Scholar-Practitioner

The residency affirms the historic vision of the pastor as both theologian and practitioner. Pastors are called to know God deeply, to understand the human condition truthfully, and to apply the Gospel wisely in the varied circumstances of ministry.

Residents are therefore encouraged to cultivate lifelong habits of reading, reflection, and disciplined spiritual devotion. Intellectual formation serves pastoral love. Theological clarity strengthens pastoral care. Spiritual maturity sustains pastoral endurance.

As the apostle Paul exhorted Timothy:

"Practice these things, immerse yourself in them, so that all may see your progress."

—1 Timothy 4:15

Mentored Formation

A distinguishing feature of the Shepherd's Path Residency is the intentional mentoring relationship between the resident and an experienced supervising pastor. Through regular meetings, theological reflection, ministry evaluation, and prayer, the mentor assists the resident in integrating knowledge, skill, and character.

This relationship reflects the apostolic pattern of formation seen in Paul and Timothy, as well as the historic pattern of apprenticeship within Christian ministry.

Mentored formation strengthens pastoral confidence while cultivating humility, wisdom, and resilience.

Formation for Enduring Ministry

The Shepherd's Path Residency is designed not merely for early success but for lifelong faithfulness. Many pastors enter ministry with strong theological preparation but limited guidance in sustaining personal health, family stability, and vocational endurance.

The Pastoral Training Model therefore seeks to preclude pastoral burnout and dropout through balanced formation that integrates:

- theological depth
- spiritual vitality
- relational health
- ministry competence
- vocational clarity

By cultivating sustainable rhythms of ministry and spiritual life, the residency contributes to the long-term flourishing of pastors and congregations.

Word and Work

The Shepherd's Path Residency affirms that pastoral ministry involves both proclamation and presence, both theological reflection and practical service.

The pastor proclaims Christ through preaching and teaching, and embodies Christ through compassionate shepherding of the flock.

Word and work belong together in faithful ministry.

Through this integration, the resident learns to shepherd God's people in the ordinary means of grace—Word, Sacrament, and Prayer—while engaging the wider mission of the Church in the world.

A Contribution to the Renewal of Pastoral Formation

The Shepherd's Path Residency represents a contribution to the renewal of pastoral education in the contemporary Church. By recovering the historic balance between academic preparation and mentored ministry practice, the Pastoral Training Model seeks to strengthen the next generation of Christian shepherds.

The prayer guiding this work echoes the apostolic hope:

"For what is our hope or joy or crown of boasting before our Lord Jesus at his coming? Is it not you?"

—1 Thessalonians 2:19

Through faithful formation, wise mentorship, and reliance upon the grace of God, the Shepherd's Path Residency seeks to serve Christ's Church by preparing pastors who will proclaim the Gospel, care for souls, and endure in ministry for the glory of God.

THE D. JAMES KENNEDY INSTITUTE
OF REFORMED LEADERSHIP

The Shepherd's Path
Pastoral Residency

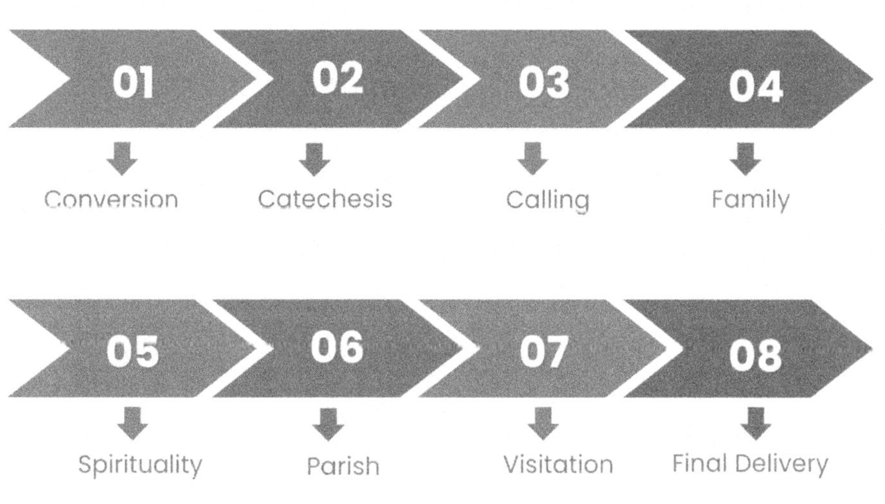

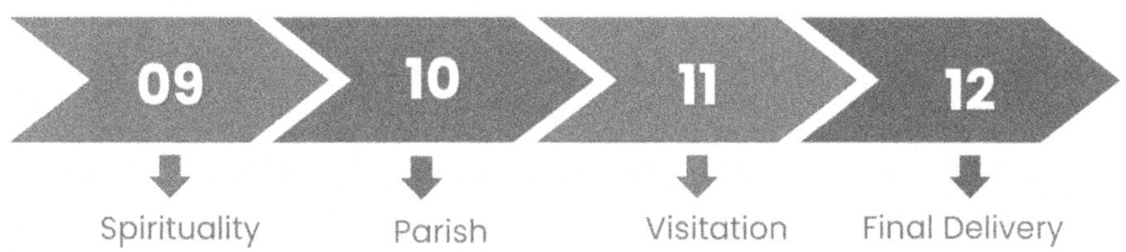

15
THE FELLOWSHIP PHASE
EARLY VOCATIONAL FORMATION AND SUPPORT

The Fellowship phase strengthens pastors during the early years of ministry by providing continued mentoring, theological reflection, and encouragement. Fellowship reinforces habits of resilience, accountability, and sustained spiritual vitality.

"Exhort one another every day… that none of you may be hardened."

—Hebrews 3:13

Through shared wisdom and continued guidance, pastors grow in confidence and perseverance.

The **Fellowship phase** extends formation beyond the Residency into the first two years of independent ministry leadership. This season is often marked by increased responsibility, vocational pressure, and the need for continued mentoring support.

Many pastors experience their greatest vulnerability during the transition from supervised ministry to full pastoral responsibility. Fellowship provides structured encouragement that strengthens resilience and promotes healthy patterns of ministry.

Fellowship may be structured formally through denominational initiatives, institute programs, or pastoral cohorts, or informally through mentoring relationships.

Common elements include:

- continued mentoring conversations
- peer cohort gatherings
- theological reflection on ministry experience
- guided spiritual discipline accountability
- leadership coaching
- vocational encouragement
- continuing education participation

During Fellowship, pastors deepen competencies first developed during Residency while navigating real-world ministry challenges such as:

- preaching preparation rhythms
- leadership of church officers
- pastoral counseling complexities
- family life balance
- time management
- congregational conflict
- evangelism leadership

- ministry vision development

Fellowship strengthens pastoral confidence while reinforcing humility and dependence upon Christ.

The aim of Fellowship is perseverance in faithful ministry and the cultivation of wisdom through experience guided by reflection and prayer.

16

LIFELONG LEARNING

CONTINUING GROWTH IN THEOLOGY, MINISTRY, AND SPIRITUAL LIFE

Lifelong Learning recognizes that pastoral formation continues throughout the minister's vocation. Faithful shepherds remain students of Scripture, theology, and the human condition as they serve Christ and His Church.

"Give attendance to reading... meditate upon these things."

—1 Timothy 4:13–15

Ongoing study deepens wisdom, strengthens ministry, and renews spiritual attentiveness.

Pastoral formation does not conclude with ordination or installation in ministry. The **Lifelong Learning phase** recognizes that the calling to shepherd Christ's flock requires continual intellectual, spiritual, and vocational development.

Faithful pastors remain students of Scripture and interpreters of human experience in light of divine revelation.

Lifelong Learning encourages each pastor to identify areas of focused development that strengthen both personal spirituality and pastoral effectiveness.

Areas of concentration may include:

- biblical theology
- preaching and homiletics
- pastoral counseling
- spiritual formation
- church revitalization
- evangelism and mission
- worship leadership
- public theology
- leadership development
- pastoral care for suffering persons

Means of continuing development may include:

- guided reading programs
- writing projects
- continuing education courses
- doctoral study
- retreats and spiritual direction
- peer learning cohorts
- ministry reflection journals
- sabbatical study

The Lifelong Learning phase reinforces habits of disciplined study, theological reflection, and spiritual attentiveness.

The apostle Paul exhorted Timothy:

“Give attendance to reading, to exhortation, to doctrine... continue in them.”

—1 Timothy 4:13–16 (KJV)

Such diligence cultivates maturity that strengthens ministry across decades of service.

17
THE KEEPER OF MEANING PHASE
MENTORING THE NEXT GENERATION OF SHEPHERDS

The Keeper of Meaning represents the mature pastor who transmits wisdom gained through years of ministry. Through mentoring relationships, seasoned shepherds contribute to the continuity of faithful pastoral leadership within the Church.

"Commit these things to faithful men who will be able to teach others also."

—2 Timothy 2:2

Wisdom received becomes wisdom shared.

The final phase of the Pastoral Training Model recognizes the unique calling of seasoned pastors to mentor the next generation.

The **Keeper of Meaning** represents the mature shepherd who preserves and transmits theological wisdom, pastoral insight, and vocational encouragement gained through years of ministry.

Throughout the history of the Church, experienced pastors have served as guides to younger ministers. The apostolic pattern of Paul and Timothy demonstrates that ministry wisdom is often transmitted through personal relationships.

The Keeper of Meaning:

- mentors younger pastors
- provides vocational counsel
- models perseverance in ministry
- transmits theological wisdom
- encourages spiritual maturity
- strengthens ministerial identity
- preserves institutional memory
- promotes continuity of faithful doctrine

Senior pastors contribute uniquely to the health of the Church by helping younger ministers interpret ministry challenges through the lens of theological truth and pastoral experience.

The role of Keeper of Meaning reflects the biblical pattern:

> "The things that thou hast heard of me... commit thou to faithful men, who shall be able to teach others also."
>
> —2 Timothy 2:2 (KJV)

The Keeper of Meaning embodies the continuity of pastoral formation across generations.

Wisdom received becomes wisdom shared.

APPENDIX 1

THE SHEPHERD'S PATH PASTORAL RESIDENCY: A TYPICAL MONTH IN THE PASTORAL RESIDENCY

The D. James Kennedy Institute's Pastoral Residency equips newly ordained men to lead as shepherds through a year-long program of practical, parish-based training. Rooted in the biblical call for men to teach and govern the church (1 Timothy 2:11–15), the Residency integrates theological reflection with hands-on ministry. Below is a typical month in the Residency, illustrating how a pastor develops one of the 12 essential competencies (e.g., preaching, counseling, prayer) under the guidance of a mentor and the church community, fostering growth in both Word and Work.

A Month in the Residency: A Relational Journey

Each month, the resident pastor engages in a structured yet relational process, blending online learning, supervised ministry, and feedback from his community. Grounded in the *Pastoral Lifecycle*'s "Growing" phase (Acts 13:13), this rhythm ensures competencies are not merely studied but lived out in the parish, reflecting the biblical model of mentorship (2 Timothy 2:1–2).

1 Engage the Lecture:

◦ The month begins with a video lecture by a Senior Fellow (e.g., Dr. George Grant on prayer, *Pastoral Residency Syllabus*, page 4). The pastor watches the session, taking notes on the competency (e.g., cultivating a prayerful life) and its application to ministry.

◦ *Purpose*: Anchors the pastor in sound doctrine, aligning with *A Theology of Learning*'s call for learning as worship (page 33).

2 Begin Reading:

◦ The pastor selects a book from the Residency bibliography (e.g., on preaching or pastoral care) to complete before the program's end. He begins reading, applying insights to his ministry tasks.

◦ *Purpose*: Deepens theological and practical understanding, fostering "deep learning" (*A Theology of Learning*, pages 19–20).

3 Download Monthly Goals:

◦ The pastor downloads the Residency goals for the month's competency (*Pastoral Residency Syllabus*, page 3), outlining specific tasks (e.g., prepare a sermon, visit a congregant). These guide his parish work.

◦ *Purpose*: Provides clear objectives, ensuring intentional growth in the competency.

4 Meet with the Supervisor:

◦ The pastor meets with his designated pastoral supervisor, typically a seasoned pastor, to discuss the competency and plan its application (e.g., leading a prayer service). The meeting begins and ends with prayer and lasts no longer than 30 minutes, often over a meal.

◦ *Purpose*: Reflects Paul's mentorship model (2 Timothy 2:1–2), ensuring biblical guidance for male leadership (1 Timothy 2:13).

5 Apply the Competency in Ministry:

◦ The pastor applies the competency in his congregation—perhaps preaching a sermon or counseling a member—under the supervisor's oversight. He records a verbatim, a detailed account of a ministry interaction (e.g., a counseling session), capturing dialogue and reflections.

◦ *Purpose*: Grounds learning in real ministry, aligning with the PTM's parish-based model.

6 Seek Feedback from the Residency Team:

◦ The pastor shares his verbatim with four team members, each offering unique perspectives, with meetings beginning and ending in prayer and lasting no more than 30 minutes:

▪ **Peer (Another Pastor)**: A fellow pastor reflects on the competency's relevance to early ministry, sharing insights from his experience.

▪ **Layman**: A male lay leader considers how the competency serves the church's discipleship and evangelism, ensuring community impact.

▪ **Wife (or Older Woman)**: If married, the pastor's wife reflects on how the competency affects women in the church and family life, aligning with her role as a helper (1 Timothy 2:10, 5:14). If single, an older woman (at least old enough to be his mother) offers maternal wisdom, as per Titus 2:3–4.

▪ **Supervisor (Wrap-Up)**: The pastor returns to his supervisor, sharing feedback received, refining his approach, and closing with prayer.

◦ *Purpose*: Fosters a relational, community-driven approach, valuing diverse perspectives while upholding male leadership (1 Timothy 2:12).

Why This Matters

This monthly rhythm embodies the D. James Kennedy Institute's vision of forming male pastors who lead with biblical authority and pastoral care. By integrating online learning, supervised ministry, and feedback from peers, laymen, and women in biblically appropriate roles, the Residency ensures pastors grow as shepherds who honor God's design for the church. For newly ordained men, it offers a practical path to competence; for congregations, it promises leaders equipped for Word and Work, rooted in the grace of Christ Jesus (2 Timothy 2:1).

APPENDIX 2
THE SHEPHERD'S PATH PASTORAL RESIDENCY: VERBATIM GUIDE AND SAMPLE

Adapted from: Michael A. Milton, "A Guide to Writing a Verbatim in Pastoral Care and Counseling Class".[1]

PURPOSE

A Verbatim is a written record that documents the dialogue and events of a ministry event in pastoral settings. It captures the details of the event—actual dialogue, actions, and emotions—so that the resident can reflect on what happened, what was learned, and how to improve.

STRUCTURE OF A VERBATIM

1 Introduction

- Date, context, purpose of the ministry event.
- Identify participants (using pseudonyms).

2 Narrative/Transcript

- Record dialogue in as much detail as possible.
- Include non-verbal cues (tone, body language).

3 Analysis

- Theological reflection: What doctrines, Scriptures, or confessional truths were engaged?
- Pastoral reflection: What worked? What could be improved?
- Emotional reflection: How did the resident feel, and how did the participant(s) likely feel?

4 Conclusion

- Lessons learned.
- Questions raised for further discussion.
- Connection to the pastoral competency.

SAMPLE VERBATIM (ABBREVIATED)

Competency: Pastoral Care in Times of Illness

Event: Hospital visitation of a church member

Date: June 3, 2025

Introduction

The pastoral resident visited Mr. S. (pseudonym), a 68-year-old member hospitalized for surgery. Purpose: to provide Christian spiritual care, i.e., soul comfort, prayer, and encouragement.

Transcript (excerpt)

• Resident: "Mr. S., I'm here to pray with you before your surgery. How are you feeling?"

• Mr. S.: "Honestly, Pastor, I'm afraid. I keep thinking about the worst outcome."

• Resident: "That is understandable. The Psalms remind us, 'When I am afraid, I put my trust in you' (Ps. 56:3)."

• (Mr. S. bows his head, visibly teary-eyed.)

• Resident: "Would it help if I read Psalm 23 together with you?"

Analysis

• **Theological**: Brought Scripture into the moment, grounded in God's sovereignty and comfort.

• **Pastoral**: Patient's fear was acknowledged before offering Scripture, which opened a path for authentic pastoral care.

• **Emotional**: Resident noted personal nervousness but overcame it by leaning on Scripture.

Conclusion

• Lesson: Active listening is essential before offering counsel.

• Questions for reflection: Did the Scripture connect deeply? How might prayer have been more participatory?

• Link to Competency: Demonstrated essential skill of bringing God's Word into times of suffering.

APPENDIX 3
THE SHEPHERD'S PATH PASTORAL RESIDENCY: REFLECTION QUESTIONS BY MONTHLY PASTORAL COMPETENCY

1. CONVERSION (EVANGELISM & NEW BIRTH)

Supervisor

1 How did the resident's ministry in this event present the gospel with clarity and fidelity?

2 Did the resident balance proclamation with pastoral sensitivity?

3 How might the church better support ongoing evangelism flowing from this encounter?

Lay Leader

1 How did this ministry moment strengthen our congregation's evangelistic witness?

2 What obstacles do you see in our community to hearing the gospel?

3 How could lay leaders partner with the resident in future outreach?

Peer

1 How does early ministry test one's confidence in evangelism?

2 What practices sustain boldness without arrogance?

3 Looking back, what do you wish you had done differently in presenting the gospel?

Wife/Motherly Figure

1 How does a husband/father's evangelistic ministry shape family life?

2 How can the family guard against discouragement when conversions are not immediate?

3 What role does hospitality and home life play in evangelism?

2. CATECHISM (TEACHING THE FAITH)

Supervisor

1 Was doctrine taught clearly, accessibly, and faithfully?

2 Did the resident connect catechesis to worship and daily life?

3 How might the resident improve in leading others into doctrinal formation?

Lay Leader

1 How did this teaching strengthen the congregation's grasp of faith?

2 What age groups or segments of the church most need catechesis?

3 How can lay leaders extend teaching into small groups or homes?

Peer

1 What challenges did you face in teaching doctrine early in ministry?

2 How do you balance depth with accessibility?

3 What practical tools have helped you teach the faith?

Wife/Motherly Figure

1 How can doctrinal teaching bless or burden family rhythms?

2 How might the resident's teaching at church flow naturally into the home?

3 How do you perceive the spiritual growth of the family through catechesis?

3. CALLING (DISCERNMENT & VOCATION)

Supervisor

1 Did the resident demonstrate clarity about his pastoral call?

2 How does this event reveal strengths or weaknesses in his sense of vocation?

3 How might the congregation affirm or challenge this call?

Lay Leader

1 How can the church discern and support genuine callings?

2 Did the resident's ministry strengthen your confidence in his vocation?

3 How can lay leaders model vocational faithfulness in their spheres?

Peer

1 What struggles did you face in discerning your call?

2 How did you confirm your vocation over time?

3 How should one respond when doubts about calling arise?

Wife/Motherly Figure

1 How does a pastoral calling affect marriage and family life?

2 What sacrifices has this calling required of you?

3 How do you experience God's confirmation of your husband's call?

4. FAMILY (MARRIAGE, CHILDREN, HOUSEHOLD)

Supervisor

1 Did the resident balance family responsibilities with ministry duties?

2 How might the church help protect pastoral family time?

3 What lessons did this competency reveal for family discipleship?

Lay Leader

1 How does the resident model a healthy Christian family life?

2 How can lay families learn from and support the pastor's family?

3 What family-related ministries could be strengthened?

Peer

1 What early mistakes did you make in balancing family and ministry?

2 How have you protected family life in the long run?

3 What encouragement would you give this resident for family faithfulness?

Wife/Motherly Figure

1 What has been most challenging in balancing ministry and home?

2 How does the church support or strain your family?

3 What has brought joy to your family life in ministry?

5. SPIRITUALITY (PERSONAL DEVOTION & PRAYER)

Supervisor

1 Did the resident show evidence of a disciplined devotional life?

2 How was spirituality integrated into public ministry?

3 Where might growth be encouraged in prayer and devotion?

Lay Leader

1 Did you observe authentic spiritual vitality in the resident?

2 How can lay leaders be encouraged toward deeper personal devotion?

3 What practices seemed most contagious for the congregation?

Peer

1 How did you struggle with spiritual dryness in early ministry?

2 What disciplines helped sustain you?

3 How do you guard against ministry replacing your walk with God?

Wife/Motherly Figure

1 How does the pastor's private devotion influence the home?

2 What ways does family life reveal strengths or weaknesses in spirituality?

3 How do you experience shared prayer in the home?

6. PARISH LIFE (COMMUNITY & CONGREGATIONAL LEADERSHIP)

Supervisor

1 Did the resident demonstrate shepherding leadership?

2 How did he engage different groups within the church?

3 How might he grow in uniting the body of Christ?

Lay Leader

1 How does the resident connect with the congregation's needs?

2 What parish concerns require more pastoral attention?

3 How might the church's community life be strengthened?

Peer

1 What were your early struggles in building congregational trust?

2 How did you learn to navigate parish conflicts?

3 How can a young minister cultivate a culture of love?

Wife/Motherly Figure

1 How does parish life affect your family rhythms?

2 Where do you feel most supported by the congregation?

3 What challenges are most pressing for the pastor's family in parish life?

7. VISITATION (MINISTRY OF PRESENCE, PASTORAL CARE)

Supervisor

1 Did the resident demonstrate empathy and biblical care in visitation?

2 How did he balance presence with proclamation?

3 How might his pastoral care deepen?

Lay Leader

1 How did this visit strengthen the life of the church?

2 What needs did you see met—or left unmet?

3 How can visitation be better supported by lay leaders?

Peer

1 How did you grow in visitation during early ministry?

2 What mistakes should this resident avoid?

3 How do you balance presence, prayer, and Scripture in care?

Wife/Motherly Figure

1 How does visitation impact family time and energy?

2 What blessings or burdens does visitation bring home?

3 How can the congregation help protect the pastor's family in this duty?

8. COUNSELING (SHEPHERDING THE SOUL)

Supervisor

1 Did the resident listen well and apply the gospel with discernment?

2 How did he use Scripture, prayer, and wisdom in counseling?

3 What growth areas are evident in his counseling ministry?

Lay Leader

1 How does pastoral counseling strengthen the congregation?

2 What needs are most pressing for counseling support?

3 How can lay leaders direct others appropriately to pastoral counsel?

Peer

1 What were your greatest lessons in early pastoral counseling?

2 How do you guard against overextension?

3 How do you handle situations beyond your expertise?

Wife/Motherly Figure

1 How does counseling ministry affect your home life?

2 What emotional weight does counseling bring?

3 How can the family support the pastor in this area without being burdened?

9. PREACHING (PROCLAMATION OF THE WORD)

Supervisor

1 Did the resident's sermon faithfully expound Scripture?

2 Was the delivery clear, engaging, and pastoral?

3 How might his preaching deepen in power and grace?

Lay Leader

1 How did the congregation receive the message?

2 Was it clear, biblical, and relevant?

3 How might lay leaders reinforce the preached Word?

Peer

1 What struggles did you face in early preaching?

2 How do you manage feedback and criticism?

3 What practices sustain growth as a preacher?

Wife/Motherly Figure

1 How does sermon preparation affect family life?

2 What burdens and joys do you observe in your husband's preaching?

3 How do you see the preached Word shaping your family?

10. THE WORD (SCRIPTURE IN MINISTRY)

Supervisor

1 Did the resident use Scripture faithfully across ministry tasks?

2 How did he handle the Word in private and public contexts?

3 Where might his biblical ministry be deepened?

Lay Leader

1 How did Scripture guide this ministry moment?

2 How might the church grow in Scripture-saturation?

3 How can lay leaders better embody the Word?

Peer

1 How did you learn to handle Scripture responsibly in early ministry?

2 What dangers exist in neglecting the Word?

3 How do you keep Scripture central in all pastoral work?

Wife/Motherly Figure

1 How does Scripture in ministry shape your home life?

2 How do you and your family engage the Word together?

3 How do you see God's Word sustaining your family?

11. SACRAMENTS (BAPTISM & LORD'S SUPPER)

Supervisor

1 Did the resident administer sacraments with reverence and biblical fidelity?

2 How did he explain the meaning to the congregation?

3 How might he improve in pastoral preparation around sacraments?

Lay Leader

1 How did the sacraments strengthen the life of the church?

2 Were they understood by the congregation?

3 How might the sacraments foster deeper fellowship?

Peer

1 What did you learn about sacraments early in ministry?

2 How do you pastorally guard against formality without meaning?

3 How do you prepare congregations for these holy ordinances?

Wife/Motherly Figure

1 How do sacraments shape your family's life of faith?

2 How do you experience these ordinances personally as part of ministry?

3 What questions do families often bring up about baptism and communion?

12. PRAYER (CORPORATE & PERSONAL INTERCESSION)

Supervisor

1 Did the resident model prayer with reverence and sincerity?

2 How was prayer integrated into ministry?

3 How might his prayer leadership be strengthened?

Lay Leader

1 How did prayer impact the congregation in this event?

2 What needs for prayer are most urgent in our community?

3 How can lay leaders encourage prayer beyond Sunday worship?

Peer

1 How did you grow in leading prayer as a young pastor?

2 What disciplines helped you lead with authenticity?

3 How do you protect against prayer becoming performance?

Wife/Motherly Figure

1 How does corporate prayer influence your home?

2 What burdens of prayer do you carry together as a family?

3 How can the church better support the family in prayer?

APPENDIX 4

THE SHEPHERD'S PATH PASTORAL RESIDENCY: THE KEEPER OF MEANING

The Pastoral Training Model will consist of four stages during active ministry. However, we recognize that vocational ministry is tied to identity. This is similar to a physician who tends to maintain the identity of a doctor even after active practice is completed. Yet, the analogy breaks down because the Christian pastor possesses a visceral and spiritual understanding of self in relationship to God as well as to mankind. The transition from Active ministry to inactive—whether it's due to retirement, aging, or disability—is fraught with potential problems. As outlined in the academic paper included in this book, this transition often leads to a higher rate of depression and other mental and behavioral health challenges. We believe these issues can be offset with a strong transition that honors the past while looking to the future. There should be a formal transition process in which the minister, along with his family, discusses financial, vocational, housing, and other concerns with professionals provided by the church and the ministry he has served. Additionally, there should be a plan for living out his role as keeper of meaning. This could include writing, part-time counseling, or mentoring other pastors in the local judicatory (district, diocese, presbytery, association). Indeed, a well-thought-out plan for his role as keeper of meaning is essential. We provide a suggested covenant between the minister and the congregation or ministry in the next heading.

A COVENANT FOR KEEPER OF MEANING

Preamble

In the name of the Triune God—Father, Son, and Holy Spirit—we enter this covenant as a sacred bond between [Minister's Name], transitioning from active ministry, and the congregation/ministry of [Church/Ministry Name]. Recognizing that vocational ministry is deeply tied to one's identity in Christ (Ephesians 4:1), akin to a physician who retains their calling beyond practice, yet uniquely spiritual in its relational depth to God and His people, we acknowledge the challenges of this shift—whether due to retirement, aging, disability, or vocational change. As research highlights, such transitions can heighten risks of depression and other trials, but we believe these can be mitigated through honor, Gospel-centered planning, and communal support. Honoring the past labors of this faithful servant (1 Timothy 5:17: "Let the elders who rule well be considered worthy of double honor, especially those who labor in preaching and teaching"), we look to the future with hope (Philippians 3:13–14: "Forgetting what lies behind and straining forward to what lies ahead, I press on toward the goal for the prize of the upward call of God in Christ Jesus"). This covenant commits us to prayerful, practical, and familial care, ensuring [Minister's Name] continues as a Keeper of Meaning, bearing fruit in old age (Psalm 92:14) as God does a new thing (Isaiah 43:18–19: "Remember not the former things, nor consider the things of old. Behold, I am doing a new thing; now it springs forth, do you not perceive it?").

Commitments of the Congregation/Ministry

We, the elders, leaders, and members of [Church/Ministry Name], covenant to:

• **Provide Prayer Support:** Establish a dedicated prayer team or network to intercede regularly for [Minister's Name] and their family, lifting up their spiritual, emotional, and physical needs (James 5:16: "The prayer of a righteous person has great power as it is working"). This may include monthly prayer gatherings, email updates for focused petitions, or a prayer calendar shared with the congregation.

• **Develop a Ministry Plan:** Collaborate with [Minister's Name] to create a personalized plan for this Keeper of Meaning season, drawing on their gifts for ongoing service—such as mentoring younger pastors in the judicatory, writing devotional resources, part-time counseling, or occasional teaching (Leviticus 19:32: "You shall stand up before the gray head and honor the face of an old man, and you shall fear your God: I am the Lord"). We will provide resources, including access to church facilities, financial stipends if feasible, and connections to denominational networks, reviewing the plan annually to adapt as needed.

• **Offer Family Support:** Extend care to [Minister's Wife's Name] and any children still at home, recognizing the shared burdens and blessings of ministry (1 Timothy 5:8: "But if anyone does not provide for his relatives, and especially for members of his household, he has denied the faith and is worse than an unbeliever"). This includes practical aid like financial counseling for retirement or housing transitions, emotional support through check-ins or counseling referrals, and social inclusion in church events to foster belonging and prevent isolation.

Commitments of the Minister

I, [Minister's Name], covenant to:

• **Receive and Engage Support:** Humbly accept the congregation's prayer and practical aid, sharing updates on needs and joys to guide their intercessions, while entrusting this transition to God's providential care (Philippians 4:6: "Do not be anxious about anything, but in everything by prayer and supplication with thanksgiving let your requests be made known to God").

• **Fulfill the Ministry Plan:** Actively participate in shaping and living out my role as Keeper of Meaning, offering wisdom to the next generation through mentoring, writing, or other avenues, as health and circumstances allow, always pointing to Christ's Gospel (Titus 2:2: "Older men are to be sober-minded, dignified, self-controlled, sound in faith, in love, and in steadfastness").

• **Care for Family:** Prioritize the well-being of my wife and family, involving them in transition discussions and seeking communal support to nurture our home as a haven of grace (Ephesians 5:25: "Husbands, love your wives, as Christ loved the church and gave himself up for her").

Mutual Affirmations

We affirm together that this covenant is rooted in the Gospel—Christ's finished work that redeems our past, sustains our present, and secures our future (Hebrews 13:8: "Jesus Christ is the same yesterday and today and forever"). We commit to reviewing this agreement annually, amending as needed in prayerful discernment, and resolving any concerns through biblical mediation. May this bond glorify God, edify His Church, and bring peace to all involved.

Signatures

[Minister's Name] ______________________ Date: ________

[Minister's Spouse's Name, if applicable] ______________________
Date: ________

[Church Elder/Representative] ______________________ Date: ________

[Additional Witnesses, e.g., Judicatory Leader] ______________________ Date: ________

A LITURGY FOR TRANSITION INTO KEEPER OF MEANING

The current pastor welcomes everyone and provides a brief overview of the pastoral training model and the intentional transition to "Keeper of Meaning." Alternatively, this may be printed in a bulletin.

The suggested welcome and briefing follows:

Beloved congregation, family, and friends—grace and peace to you in the name of our Lord Jesus Christ.

Today, we gather not in sorrow but in joyful thanksgiving to mark a sacred transition in the life of our dear brother/sister [Minister's Name]. As many of you know, the Pastoral Training Model (PTM) of the D. James Kennedy Institute of Reformed Leadership offers a comprehensive pathway for equipping God's servants—from Internship and Residency in the early stages of development to Fellowship and Lifelong Learning in sustained ministry. It restores the ancient wisdom of apprenticeship by combining rigorous theological education with hands-on service, all aimed at combating the isolation and burnout that can shadow our calling.

Yet, the PTM wisely extends beyond active ministry years, culminating in the Keeper of Meaning—a season where experienced shepherds like [Minister's Name] share their wisdom with the next generation, much as Paul mentored Timothy from prison (2 Timothy

2:2). This intentional transition honors the past labors that have borne fruit among us (1 Timothy 5:17) while looking forward to God's new mercies (Isaiah 43:19). Whether prompted by age, retirement, disability, or a change in vocation, we, as a church body, commit to supporting [Minister's Name] and their family through prayer, practical care, and opportunities to share their legacy—ensuring they continue to glorify Christ in this fruitful chapter.

Let us now enter this liturgy with hearts full of praise, celebrating the Chief Shepherd who leads us through every season (1 Peter 5:4).

Call to Worship (Led by the Presiding Minister)

Minister: Beloved in Christ, we gather in the name of the Father, Son, and Holy Spirit to honor God's faithful servant, [Minister's Name], as they transition into the Keeper of Meaning—a season of wisdom-sharing and legacy-bearing, as modeled by the Apostle Paul in his later letters (2 Timothy 4:6–8). Let us rejoice that our Lord, who began a good work in [Minister's Name], will carry it to completion (Philippians 1:6).

This is the day that the Lord has made; let us rejoice and be glad in it (Psalm 118:24 ESV).

All: **Thanks be to God, who gives us the victory through our Lord Jesus Christ!** (1 Corinthians 15:57)

Opening Hymn: "O God, Our Help in Ages Past" (Hymn #30 from Trinity Hymnal, 1990; Tune: ST. ANNE. Sing verses 1, 2, and 5.)

1 O God, our help in ages past, our hope for years to come, our shelter from the stormy blast, and our eternal home.

2 Under the shadow of thy throne thy saints have dwelt secure; sufficient is thine arm alone, and our defense is sure.

3 Time, like an ever-rolling stream, bears all its sons away; they fly, forgotten, as a dream dies at the opening day.

Scripture Readings (Read by Family Members or Colleagues)

• *From the Old Testament:* "The righteous flourish like the palm tree and grow like a cedar in Lebanon... In old age they still produce fruit; they are always green and full of sap" (Psalm 92:12, 14, ESV).

• *From the New Testament:* "For I am already being poured out as a drink offering, and the time of my departure has come. I have fought the good fight, I have finished the race, I have kept the faith. Henceforth there is laid up for me the crown of righteousness, which the Lord, the righteous judge, will award to me on that day" (2 Timothy 4:6–8, ESV).

• *Gospel Proclamation:* "Well done, good and faithful servant. You have been faithful over a little; I will set you over much. Enter into the joy of your master" (Matthew 25:21, ESV).

Prayer of Thanksgiving and Commissioning (Led by a Fellow Pastor or Elder)

O LORD OUT GOD, Giver of every good gift, we thank You for the Gospel of grace that called [Minister's Name] into Your service and sustained him [and his wife and family] through [number] years of faithful ministry. As they enter this Keeper of Meaning phase—whether by the gentle turning of age, the rest of retirement, the trials of disability, or a new vocational path—we praise You for the fruit borne in Your Kingdom.

Lord Jesus, our Great High Priest, honor this servant as we honor You. Proclaim afresh the Gospel through their legacy: that Christ died for our sins, rose victorious, and reigns eternally. Grant [Minister's Name] and their family peace in this transition, surrounding them with Your Church's support—through prayer, fellowship, and practical care. Help them to share wisdom with younger generations, as Paul mentored Timothy, that Your truth may endure.

Holy Spirit, equip us all to finish well. In the name of Jesus Christ, our Lord, who reigns with You, O Father, and the Holy Spirit, one God, world without end. Amen.

Affirmations and Support Commitments (Shared by Congregation, Family, and Colleagues)

• *From the Congregation/Judicatory:* "We affirm your faithful service, [Minister's Name], and commit to honoring your wisdom as a Keeper of Meaning. We pledge ongoing prayer, visitation, and resources to support you and your family in this season."

• *From the Family:* "We give thanks for God's sustaining grace and commit to walking this transition together, seeking His joy in rest and reflection."

• *From Peers/Younger Ministers:* "We receive your mantle of wisdom with gratitude, pledging to learn from your experiences and carry forward the Gospel mission."

(Invite brief, prepared testimonies or symbols, such as presenting a Bible inscribed with 2 Timothy 2:2.)

Pastoral Prayer

Closing Hymn: "How Firm a Foundation" (Hymn #94 from Trinity Hymnal, 1990; Tune: FOUNDATION. Sing verses 1, 2, and 5.)

1 How firm a foundation, you saints of the Lord, is laid for your faith in his excellent Word! What more can he say than to you he has said, to you who for refuge to Jesus have fled?

2 "Fear not, I am with you, O be not dismayed, for I am your God, and will still give you aid; I'll strengthen you, help you, and cause you to stand, upheld by my righteous, omnipotent hand."

3 "E'en down to old age all my people shall prove my sovereign, eternal, unchangeable love; and when hoary hairs shall their temples adorn, like lambs they shall still in my bosom be borne."

Benediction (By the Keeper of Meaning pastor if possible)

---

* A Fellowship time follows.

APPENDIX 5
COVENANTS (AGREEMENTS)

1. INTERNSHIP COVENANT

This covenant serves as a formal agreement between the intern, supervising pastor, and congregation, outlining commitments during the Internship phase (grounded in supervised parish application and assessment, as per the PTM summary).

Pastoral Internship Covenant

D. James Kennedy Institute of Reformed Leadership

Date: [Insert Date]

We, the undersigned, enter into this covenant in the spirit of mutual edification and faithful service to Christ's Church, guided by the authority of Scripture (2 Timothy 3:16–17) and our shared Reformed confessions. This covenant governs the Internship phase of the Pastoral Training Model (PTM), integrating theological education with practical ministry.

Intern's Commitments:

• I, [Intern's Name], a student pursuing theological education, commit to:

◦ Engage diligently in supervised parish ministry, applying seminary coursework to real-world tasks such as preaching, pastoral care, and visitation.

◦ Participate in weekly meetings with my supervisor for reflection, feedback, and spiritual accountability.

◦ Submit verbatim reports of ministry encounters for evaluation, seeking growth in the PTM's competencies (e.g., Conversion and Calling, Preaching the Word).

◦ Uphold the values of the Institute, including the inerrancy of Scripture and multimodal learning through apprenticeship.

◦ Maintain confidentiality, humility, and a prayerful posture in all interactions.

Supervising Pastor's Commitments:

• I, [Supervising Pastor's Name], as the designated mentor, commit to:

◦ Provide at least one hour weekly of direct supervision, offering guidance rooted in biblical wisdom and Reformed doctrine.

◦ Oversee the intern's integration of classroom study with parish practice, ensuring exposure to diverse ministry experiences.

◦ Evaluate the intern's progress quarterly, providing constructive feedback aligned with PTM goals.

◦ Model pastoral identity and resilience, praying regularly for the intern's formation.

Congregation's Commitments:

• We, the elders and members of [Church Name], commit to:

- Welcome the intern as a fellow servant, providing opportunities for ministry involvement and feedback.

- Support the intern through prayer, hospitality, and resources, fostering a community of growth.

- Respect the learning process, offering grace in successes and challenges.

This covenant shall remain in effect for [Duration, e.g., one academic year] or until mutually amended. We sign in faith, trusting God to equip us for every good work (2 Timothy 3:17).

Signatures:

[Intern] ______________________ Date: ________

[Supervising Pastor] ______________________ Date: ________

[Church Elder/Representative] ______________________ Date: ________

2. Letter to the Judicatory

This letter informs the denominational body (e.g., presbytery) of the candidate's participation in the PTM, requesting endorsement and alignment with ordination processes.

Sample Letter to the Judicatory

[D. James Kennedy Institute Letterhead]

[Your Address]

[Date]

[Judicatory Leader's Name]

[Judicatory Address]

Dear [Rev./Dr. Last Name],

Grace and peace to you in our Lord Jesus Christ.

I write on behalf of the D. James Kennedy Institute of Reformed Leadership to inform you of [Candidate's Name]'s enrollment in the Pastoral Training Model (PTM), a comprehensive program designed to unite rigorous theological education with intentional pastoral apprenticeship. Rooted in historic Reformed principles and Scripture's mandate for equipping servants (Ephesians 4:11–12), the PTM addresses pastoral burnout through phased formation: Internship, Residency, Fellowship, Lifelong Learning, and Keeper of Meaning.

[Candidate's Name], under the supervision of [Supervising Pastor's Name] at [Church Name], will begin the Internship phase, integrating seminary studies with supervised ministry. This aligns with our shared commitment to the Westminster Standards and prepares candidates for faithful ordination. We kindly request your endorsement of this training, including any necessary oversight for licensure or candidacy. Enclosed are details of the PTM phases and competencies.

We value your partnership in raising up resilient shepherds for Christ's flock. Please contact me at [Your Contact Info] to discuss further.

In His service,

Dr. Michael A. Milton

President, D. James Kennedy Institute of Reformed Leadership

3. Letter to the Supervising Pastor

This letter invites and outlines expectations for the pastor overseeing the Internship or Residency phase.

Sample Letter to the Supervising Pastor

[D. James Kennedy Institute Letterhead]

[Date]

[Supervising Pastor's Name]

[Church Address]

Dear [Rev. Last Name],

May the Lord's peace be with you as you shepherd His people.

It is with great joy that I invite you to serve as Supervising Pastor for [Intern/Resident's Name] in the Pastoral Training Model (PTM) of the D. James Kennedy Institute. Your seasoned ministry and commitment to Reformed doctrine make you an ideal mentor for this formative phase.

The PTM recovers the biblical apprenticeship model (e.g., Paul and Timothy in 2 Timothy 2:2), blending education and formation to combat pastoral burnout. In the [Internship/Residency] phase, you will:

• Provide weekly supervision (1 hour), focusing on reflection and competency development (e.g., the 12 Pastoral Competencies).

• Guide hands-on ministry, including verbatim evaluations and spiritual accountability.

• Submit quarterly assessments to the Institute.

Enclosed are guidelines, a covenant template, and resources. We pray this role will bless both you and the candidate. Please confirm your participation by [Date] at [Contact Info].

Gratefully in Christ,

Dr. Michael A. Milton

President

4. Congregational Covenant

This covenant engages the church body in supporting the intern/resident, fostering a communal commitment.

Congregational Covenant for Pastoral Training

D. James Kennedy Institute of Reformed Leadership

We, the congregation of [Church Name], covenant together to support [Intern/Resident's Name] in the Pastoral Training Model (PTM), recognizing our role in equipping God's servants (Hebrews 13:17).

As a body:

- We commit to pray regularly for the intern/resident's growth and ministry.

- We will provide opportunities for service, offering gracious feedback and encouragement.

- We pledge to uphold the Institute's values, including Scripture's authority and multimodal apprenticeship.

- We will respect the learning process, extending hospitality and patience.

In return, we trust the Lord to use this partnership for our mutual edification and the advancement of His Kingdom.

Affirmed by:

[Elders' Signatures] ______________________ Date: ________

[Congregational Affirmation: e.g., Signed Petition or Vote Date]

Individual Page: (1) The Pastoral Supervisor During Internship

This one-page guide outlines roles and best practices for supervisors, drawing from seminary models like Union Presbyterian.

Guide for Pastoral Supervisors: Internship Phase

Role Overview: As supervisor, you embody the PTM's apprenticeship model, guiding the intern in integrating seminary learning with parish practice (Mark 3:14).

Key Responsibilities:

• Weekly 1-hour meetings: Discuss ministry experiences, review verbatims, and pray together.

• Exposure to competencies: Assign tasks in preaching, care, and visitation.

• Evaluations: Provide quarterly feedback on progress toward PTM goals.

• Spiritual Mentorship: Model resilience and devotion, addressing burnout risks.

Best Practices:

• Foster a safe space for reflection and growth.

• Align with Institute values (e.g., Westminster Confession).

• Collaborate with the congregation for holistic support.

Contact the Institute for resources or questions. Thank you for investing in future shepherds!

RESIDENCY, FELLOWSHIP, LIFELONG LEARNING, AND KEEPER OF MEANING

Individual Page: (2) Residency Team Members

This guide recommends team roles tailored to PTM phases, especially Residency (focusing on competencies) and beyond.

Guide for Residency Team Members: Roles by PTM Phase

Team Composition: For the Residency phase, assemble a team including the Supervising Pastor (lead), Lay Leaders (2–3), Peer Mentors (experienced pastors), and a Wife/Motherly Figure (for family insights).

Recommended Roles by Phase:

• **Residency (Growing Phase):** Focus on 12 competencies. Supervisor: Weekly oversight and evaluations. Lay Leaders: Provide congregational feedback. Peers: Share early ministry lessons. Wife/Motherly Figure: Offer perspectives on family balance.

• **Fellowship (Mentoring Phase):** Expand to include DMin advisors for specialized research; peers for peer learning communities.

• **Lifelong Learning (Reflecting Phase):** Team evolves to include online cohort facilitators and retreat leaders for ongoing renewal.

• **Keeper of Meaning:** Involve elders and younger pastors for wisdom-sharing and legacy mentoring.

General Expectations: Pray, evaluate monthly, and align with Scripture (2 Timothy 2:2). Your input fosters resilient ministry—thank you for this sacred service!

APPENDIX 6
THE SHEPHERD'S PATH PASTORAL RESIDENCY: SAMPLE INVITATION LETTER FOR RESIDENCY TEAM MEMBERS

Purpose of This Appendix

In the Residency phase of the Pastoral Training Model (PTM), the newly ordained minister (pastoral resident) works closely with the supervising pastor to assemble a Residency Team. This team provides diverse perspectives on the resident's growth in the twelve pastoral competencies, fostering accountability, encouragement, and practical wisdom. The team typically includes:

• The Supervising Pastor (lead mentor).

• A Lay Leader, who considers the impact on the local church (e.g., "How does this affect the congregation's life and mission?").

• A Peer (an experienced pastor), who shares personal insights (e.g., "Here's what I have experienced in similar ministry challenges").

• The Resident's Wife (if married) or, if single, a mature woman at least the age of the resident's mother, who offers perspectives on family and women's concerns (e.g., "How does this ministry event affect women, children, or the pastor's family?").

The following sample letter can be customized and sent by the resident and supervising pastor to invite these individuals. It emphasizes the team's role in supporting resilient, Gospel-centered ministry, as outlined in 2 Timothy 2:2: "And what you have heard from me in the presence of many witnesses entrust to faithful men, who will be able to teach others also."

Sample Invitation Letter

[Church or Institute Letterhead]

[Date]

[Invitee's Name]

[Invitee's Address]

Dear [Invitee's Name],

Grace and peace to you in our Lord Jesus Christ.

As the Supervising Pastor [or Newly Ordained Resident] in the Pastoral Training Model (PTM) of the D. James Kennedy Institute of Reformed Leadership, I/we write with great joy to invite you to serve on the Residency Team for [Resident's Name], our newly ordained pastoral resident. The PTM is a research-driven framework that unites theological education with intentional apprenticeship, equipping ministers for sustained, burnout-resistant service through phases like Internship, Residency, Fellowship, Lifelong Learning, and Keeper of Meaning. In this Residency phase—a year of intensive, post-seminary training focused on mastering twelve pastoral competencies—we seek a team of wise counselors to provide feedback and encouragement.

Your unique perspective would be invaluable:

• **As a Lay Leader**, you would help us discern the broader impact on the local church, asking questions like, "How does this ministry event or competency affect the congregation's spiritual health, unity, and mission?" Your voice ensures the resident's growth serves the body of Christ holistically (Ephesians 4:15–16).

• **As a Peer**, drawing from your own pastoral journey, you would offer experiential insights, such as, "Here's what I have experienced in navigating similar challenges," mentoring as Paul did Timothy (2 Timothy 2:2) and fostering resilience in early ministry.

• **As the Resident's Wife [or a Mature Woman Mentor]**, you would bring essential family-oriented wisdom, reflecting on questions like, "How does this ministry event affect women, children, or the pastor's family?" This role honors the biblical call to nurture the household of faith (1 Timothy 5:8) and provides a supportive lens for balancing vocational and domestic life.

Team involvement is flexible but meaningful: typically one monthly meeting (in-person or virtual) to review the resident's verbatim reports and progress, plus occasional feedback on specific competencies. Your commitment would span the Residency year, with opportunities for prayer and mutual edification. We believe this aligns with Scripture's vision of iron sharpening iron (Proverbs 27:17), strengthening not only [Resident's Name] but our entire ministry community.

If the Lord leads you to accept, please reply by [Date] to discuss next steps. We are grateful for your prayerful consideration and the ways God has already used you in His Kingdom.

In Christ's service,

[Supervising Pastor's Name]

Supervising Pastor

[Church Name]

[Newly Ordained Resident's Name]

Pastoral Resident

APPENDIX 7
THE SHEPHERD'S PATH PASTORAL RESIDENCY: THE RESIDENCY TEAM IN THE SHEPHERD'S PATH RESIDENCY

Overview and Purpose

The Residency Team is a vital component of the Residency phase in the Pastoral Training Model (PTM) of the D. James Kennedy Institute of Reformed Leadership. This phase, typically the first year post-seminary and ordination, focuses on mastering the twelve pastoral competencies through supervised ministry, hybrid learning, and reflective evaluation. The team's purpose is to provide diverse, Gospel-centered perspectives that enrich the resident's formation, fostering resilience against burnout and equipping them for lifelong service (2 Timothy 2:2: "And what you have heard from me in the presence of many witnesses entrust to faithful men, who will be able to teach others also"). This emphasis on resilience prepares us for the challenges of lifelong service.

By drawing on the insights of a supervising pastor, lay leader, peer, and family-oriented mentor, the team ensures the resident's growth is not isolated but communal, reflecting the body's interconnectedness in Christ (1 Corinthians 12:12–27). The team meets monthly to review verbatim reports of ministry encounters, offering feedback that integrates theological depth with practical wisdom. This commitment to the resident's growth reassures us of the team's unwavering support.

Team Members and Roles

The Residency Team is intentionally diverse, representing key constituencies in ministry. Each member brings a unique lens to the resident's development, ensuring balanced counsel rooted in Scripture and experience. This diversity enriches the team's perspectives, broadening our understanding of pastoral ministry.

• **Supervising Pastor (Team Lead)**: A seasoned pastor, often from the resident's church or judicatory, who oversees the team's process. Their role is to facilitate meetings, provide direct mentorship on competencies (e.g., preaching, pastoral care), and ensure alignment with PTM values like the authority of Scripture and Reformed confessions. They guide the resident in integrating feedback, modeling pastoral identity and spiritual accountability. The supervising pastor plays a crucial role in the resident's development, providing guidance, support, and a model of pastoral leadership (Titus 2:7–8: 'Show yourself in all respects to be a model of good works, and in your teaching show integrity, dignity').

• **Lay Leader**: A committed church member (elder, deacon, or active layperson) who represents the congregation's perspective. Their focus is on the local church's well-being, asking, "How does this ministry event or competency affect the congregation's spiritual health, unity, and mission?" They offer insights into how the resident's actions impact everyday believers, ensuring ministry remains grounded in service to the body (Ephesians 4:11–12: "He gave... pastors and teachers, to equip the saints for the work of ministry").

• **Peer**: An experienced pastor (ideally 5–10 years in ministry) who shares from personal journeys. Their role is to provide empathetic, practical advice, such as, 'Here's what I have experienced in navigating similar challenges,' drawing on lessons from successes and trials. This fosters peer-to-peer encouragement, helping the resident avoid common pitfalls and build resilience. The peer's role is to provide a unique perspective based on their own experiences, fostering a sense of camaraderie and shared learning (Proverbs 27:17: 'Iron sharpens iron, and one man sharpens another').

• **Wife or Mature Woman Mentor**: If the resident is married, their wife; if single, a godly woman at least the age of the resident's mother (e.g., a seasoned church member or widow). Their perspective centers on family and relational dynamics, reflecting on questions like, 'How does this ministry event affect women, children, or the pastor's family?' This role honors the holistic impact of ministry on the home, promoting balance and care. The wife or mature woman mentor plays a unique role in the resident's development, providing insights and guidance from a family perspective (1 Timothy 5:8: 'But if anyone does not provide for his relatives, and especially for members of his household, he has denied the faith').

Delimitations

To maintain a safe, edifying environment, all team discussions are governed by pastoral confidentiality, akin to the sacred trust in counseling or elder deliberations (Proverbs 11:13: "Whoever goes about slandering reveals secrets, but he who is trustworthy in spirit keeps a thing covered"). Conversations are delimited to constructive feedback on the resident's ministry practice, intended solely to help them conduct their calling in light of the constituency each member represents—whether the local church, peer experiences, or family concerns. The team does not engage in formal discipline, psychological therapy, or decisions outside the PTM's scope; any sensitive issues are referred to the supervising pastor or judicatory for appropriate handling. This ensures the focus remains on Gospel-centered growth, not judgment, fostering an atmosphere of grace and mutual building up (Ephesians 4:29: "Let no corrupting talk come out of your mouths, but only such as is good for building up").

Time Commitment

Participation is designed to be sustainable and respectful of each member's calling, requiring about thirty minutes per month—typically one virtual or in-person meeting to review the resident's progress and provide brief feedback. If optional lunches or informal gatherings occur for deeper fellowship, the resident covers the cost, which is expensed to the ministry or local church as part of the PTM's investment in formation. This modest commitment reflects the biblical principle of stewardship (1 Corinthians 4:2: "It is required of stewards that they be found faithful"), allowing team members to contribute meaningfully without undue burden.

In summary, the Residency Team embodies the PTM's vision of integrated, relational training—surrounding emerging pastors with a cloud of witnesses (Hebrews 12:1) to prepare them for fruitful, enduring ministry. Through prayerful collaboration, this team not only supports the resident but strengthens the wider Church, to the glory of Christ.

APPENDIX 8

THE SHEPHERD'S PATH PASTORAL RESIDENCY: A SAME LEARN CONTRACT

SAMPLE LEARNING CONTRACT

The Shepherd's Path Residency

Monthly Competency Formation

Resident Name: Rev. Candidate John A. Smith

Supervising Pastor: Rev. Michael T. Shepherd, D.Min.

Residency Church or Ministry Setting: Grace Covenant Presbyterian Church

Month of Residency: Month 7

Competency Focus: Visitation (Ministry of Presence)

1. COMPETENCY DESCRIPTION

The resident develops theological understanding and practical skill in the ministry of pastoral presence through visitation of the sick, homebound, grieving, and spiritually distressed. The resident learns to apply Scripture, prayer, and compassionate listening within pastoral encounters.

> "I was sick and you visited me."
>
> —Matthew 25:36

2. LEARNING OBJECTIVES

By the conclusion of this learning period, the resident will:

1 Articulate a biblical theology of pastoral visitation grounded in the compassion of Christ.

2 Demonstrate appropriate pastoral presence in hospital, home, and hospice settings.

3 Apply Scripture and prayer appropriately within pastoral visits.

4 Reflect theologically on human suffering, illness, and mortality.

5 Develop sensitivity to emotional and spiritual needs in crisis situations.

3. LEARNING ACTIVITIES

The resident will complete the following activities:

• Read selected passages from Gregory the Great, *Pastoral Rule*, Part II (sections on pastoral care).

• Read Richard Baxter, *The Reformed Pastor*, sections on personal oversight of the flock.

• Observe the supervising pastor conducting at least three pastoral visits.

• Conduct a minimum of six supervised pastoral visits.

- Participate in one hospital visitation round.
- Record observations in a pastoral reflection journal.
- Discuss pastoral care case studies with the supervising pastor.
- Memorize and appropriately employ selected Scripture passages suitable for pastoral visitation.

4. EVIDENCE OF LEARNING

Evidence demonstrating progress in this competency will include:

- Written reflection (2–3 pages) on the theology of suffering and pastoral care
- Journal entries documenting visitation experiences
- Supervising the pastor's evaluation of the resident's pastoral presence
- Scripture passages selected for pastoral care settings
- Case reflection describing one pastoral encounter

5. MENTORING CONVERSATION SUMMARY

Date of mentoring meeting: March 18

Discussion included:

The supervising pastor affirmed the resident's ability to listen attentively and to communicate empathy appropriately. The resident demonstrated growing confidence in praying aloud with individuals who are ill. Additional encouragement was given to allow greater silence during pastoral visits and to rely more intentionally upon Scripture reading.

The supervising pastor emphasized that pastoral visitation reflects the incarnational ministry of Christ, who enters into human suffering with compassion and truth.

6. EVALUATION

Competency Progress:

☑ Developing

☑ Demonstrated growth

☐ Competency achieved

☐ Requires additional attention

Strengths observed:

- Appropriate tone and demeanor in sensitive situations
- Careful use of Scripture
- Demonstrated compassion and attentiveness

Areas for continued growth:

- Greater confidence in initiating spiritual conversation
- Continued theological reflection on suffering and hope

7. RESIDENT REFLECTION

Through these visits, I have come to understand more deeply the importance of presence in pastoral ministry. I observed that individuals facing illness often seek reassurance of God's presence rather than an extended explanation. The reading from Baxter helped me recognize that pastoral visitation is not an optional activity but central to shepherding the flock.

I was especially moved by the opportunity to pray with a hospitalized church member who expressed renewed confidence in Christ's promises. I am learning that the pastor's presence often communicates care even before words are spoken.

8. SUPERVISING PASTOR COMMENTS

The resident is developing appropriate pastoral sensitivity and demonstrates a teachable spirit. Continued experience will strengthen confidence and deepen theological understanding of pastoral care. The resident is encouraged to continue integrating Scripture naturally into conversation and prayer.

9. SIGNATURES

Resident Signature: ____________________

Date: ________

Supervising Pastor Signature: ____________________ Date: ________

APPENDIX 9
A SUMMARY FOR SHARING WITH OTHERS ABOUT THE PASTORAL TRAINING MODEL

We provide a condensed version of the pastoral training model. This can be shared when discussing the PTM, such as with judicatory members, proposed supervising pastor or pastors, family, or residency team members.

THE PASTORAL TRAINING MODEL

An Initiative of the D. James Kennedy Institute of Reformed Leadership

The **Pastoral Training Model (PTM)** is designed to sustain ministers across the **entire pastoral lifecycle**, from seminary to seasoned service. Rooted in Scripture and informed by research, the PTM unites rigorous theological formation with intentional pastoral apprenticeship.

FOUR PHASES OF THE PTM

- **Internship** – Grounding seminary training in supervised ministry.

• **Residency** – A guided first year of ministry with twelve pastoral competencies.

• **Fellowship** – Advanced renewal and specialized learning within five years.

• **Lifelong Learning** – Ongoing education and support for resilience and growth.

The PTM's goal is simple but vital: **to prevent pastoral burnout and cultivate a lifetime of faithful ministry.**

> "What you have heard from me in the presence of many witnesses entrust to faithful men, who will be able to teach others also" (2 Tim. 2:2).

To learn more, visit:

kennedyinstitute.net/pastoral-training-model

NOTES

12. FREQUENTLY ASKED QUESTIONS

1. Michael A. Milton, "A Pastoral Life Cycle from the Biblical Record of St. Paul's Ministry," *Faith for Living*, June 15, 2017, https://michaelmilton.org/2017/06/15/a-pastoral-life-cycle-based-upon-the-biblical-record-of-st-pauls-ministry/.
2. Milton, Michael A. (2022). *Reimagining Pastoral Education and Training: A Doctoral Thesis on Precluding Pastoral Burnout and Dropout through Recovery of Balance between the University Model and the Apprenticeship Model of Theological Higher Education.* figshare. Doctoral thesis. Erskine Theological Seminary. https://doi.org/10.6084/m9.figshare.19858144.v1
3. George E. Vaillant, "The Ego and Adult Development," in *The Wisdom of the Ego* (Harvard University Press, 1998), 155.

APPENDIX 2

1. Michael A. Milton, "A Guide to Writing a Verbatim in Pastoral Care and Counseling Class," Journal, *Faith for Living*, November 12, 2015, https://michaelmilton.org/2015/11/12/a-guide-to-writing-a-verbatim-in-pastoral-care-and-counseling-class/.

BIBLIOGRAPHY

FOUNDATIONS FOR THE PASTORAL TRAINING MODEL AND THE SHEPHERD'S PATH RESIDENCY

The Pastoral Training Model and the Shepherd's Path Residency draw upon the historic tradition of pastoral theology developed across the centuries of the Christian Church. From the early Church Fathers to the Reformers and Puritans, and continuing through modern pastoral scholarship, Christian ministers have been formed through a combination of theological study, spiritual formation, and practical shepherding of Christ's flock.

The works listed below are foundational sources that inform the theological vision, pedagogical structure, and pastoral competencies of the residency program. These texts provide guidance for preaching, worship, pastoral care, church leadership, evangelism, and the lifelong formation of ministers.

The bibliography also reflects the research foundations of the Pastoral Training Model itself, including doctoral research and contemporary studies related to theological education, clergy health, vocational formation, and global Christianity.

The following works represent key sources for the development of the Shepherd's Path Residency and the broader Pastoral Training Model.

PRIMARY HISTORICAL SOURCES FOR PASTORAL FORMATION

Augustine. *On Christian Doctrine*. Translated by D. W. Robertson Jr. Indianapolis: Bobbs-Merrill, 1958.

Baxter, Richard. *The Reformed Pastor*. Carlisle, PA: Banner of Truth Trust, 1974.

Bucer, Martin. *Concerning the True Care of Souls*. Translated by Peter Beale. Carlisle, PA: Banner of Truth Trust, 2009.

Calvin, John. *Institutes of the Christian Religion*. Edited by John T. McNeill. Translated by Ford Lewis Battles. 2 vols. Philadelphia: Westminster Press, 1960.

Chrysostom, John. *Six Books on the Priesthood*. Crestwood, NY: St. Vladimir's Seminary Press, 1984.

Edwards, Jonathan. *The Works of Jonathan Edwards*. New Haven: Yale University Press, 1957.

Gregory the Great. *The Book of Pastoral Rule*. Translated by George Demacopoulos. Crestwood, NY: St. Vladimir's Seminary Press, 2007.

Owen, John. *The Mortification of Sin*. Edinburgh: Banner of Truth Trust, 1967.

Perkins, William. *The Art of Prophesying*. Edinburgh: Banner of Truth Trust, 1996.

Spurgeon, Charles H. *Lectures to My Students*. Grand Rapids: Zondervan, 1954.

The Protestant Episcopal Church in the United States of America. *The Book of Common Prayer*. New York: Oxford University Press, 1928.

Safrai, S., and M. Stern, eds. *The Jewish People in the First Century: Historical Geography, Political History, Social, Cultural and Religious Life and Institutions*. Vol. 2. Compendia Rerum Iudaicarum ad Novum Testamentum. Assen: Van Gorcum; Philadelphia: Fortress, 1976.

CONTEMPORARY WORKS ON PASTORAL MINISTRY AND FORMATION

Beeke, Joel R. *Reformed Preaching: Proclaiming God's Word from the Heart of the Preacher to the Heart of His People*. Wheaton, IL: Crossway, 2018.

Beeke, Joel R., and Nick Thompson. *Pastors and Their Critics: A Guide to Coping with Criticism in the Ministry*. Phillipsburg, NJ: P&R Publishing, 2020.

Bonhoeffer, Dietrich. *Life Together*. New York: Harper & Row, 1954.

Ford, Coleman M., and Shawn J. Wilhite. *Ancient Wisdom for the Care of Souls: Learning the Art of Pastoral Ministry from the Church Fathers*. Wheaton, IL: Crossway, 2024.

Gore, R. J. *Covenant Worship: Reconsidering the Puritan Regulative Principle*. Phillipsburg, NJ: P&R Publishing, 2022.

Grant, George. *The Christian Almanac: A Comprehensive Guide to the Saints, Seasons, and Stories of the Year*. Nashville: Cumberland House, 2004.

Grant, George. *The Changing of the Guard: Biblical Principles for Political Action*. Fort Worth: Dominion Press, 1987.

Grant, George. *The Micah Mandate: Balancing the Christian Life*. Nashville: Cumberland House, 2005.

Grant, George. *The Mighty Weakness of John Knox*. Brentwood, TN: Wolgemuth & Hyatt, 1992.

Hughes, R. Kent. *Liberating Ministry from the Success Syndrome*. Wheaton, IL: Crossway, 1987.

Johnson, Terry L. *Leading in Worship: A Sourcebook for Pastors*. Grand Rapids: Eerdmans, 1996.

Johnson, Terry L. *Reformed Worship: Worship That Is According to Scripture*. Greenville, SC: Reformed Academic Press, 2000.

Kennedy, D. James. *Evangelism Explosion*. 4th ed. Wheaton, IL: Tyndale House, 1996.

Kennedy, D. James. *What If Jesus Had Never Been Born?* Nashville: Thomas Nelson, 1994.

Lloyd-Jones, D. Martyn. *Preaching and Preachers*. Grand Rapids: Zondervan, 1971.

Marsden, George M. *Jonathan Edwards: A Life*. New Haven: Yale University Press, 2003.

Oden, Thomas C. *Pastoral Theology: Essentials of Ministry*. San Francisco: Harper & Row, 1983.

Peterson, Eugene H. *Working the Angles: The Shape of Pastoral Integrity*. Grand Rapids: Eerdmans, 1987.

Reeder, Harry L., III. *From Embers to a Flame: How God Can Revitalize Your Church*. Phillipsburg, NJ: P&R Publishing, 2008.

Stott, John. *The Preacher's Portrait*. Grand Rapids: Eerdmans, 1961.

Willard, Dallas. *The Spirit of the Disciplines*. San Francisco: HarperCollins, 1988.

Willimon, William H. *Pastor: The Theology and Practice of Ordained Ministry*. Nashville: Abingdon Press, 2002.

Vaillant, George E. *Aging Well: Surprising Guideposts to a Happier Life from the Landmark Harvard Study of Adult Development*. Boston: Little, Brown and Company, 2002.

RESEARCH FOUNDATIONS FOR THE PASTORAL TRAINING MODEL

Center for the Study of Global Christianity. "Quick Facts about Global Christianity." Gordon-Conwell Theological Seminary, 2023. https://www.gordonconwell.edu/center-for-global-christianity/research/quick-facts/.

Meinzer, Chris A. "Preliminary Enrollment Data for Fall 2025 Shows Another Year of Promising Trends." The Association of Theological Schools, 2025. https://www.ats.edu/post/Preliminary-enrollment-data-for-fall-2025-shows-another-year-of-promising-trends.

Milton, Michael A. "Reimagining Pastoral Education and Training: Precluding Pastoral Burnout and Dropout through Recovery of Balance Between the University Model and the Apprenticeship Model of Theological Higher Education." Doctoral thesis, figshare, 2022. https://doi.org/10.6084/m9.figshare.19858144.v1.

Milton, Michael A. "Vocation and Reform in Public Administration." Master's thesis, University of North Carolina at Chapel Hill, 2016.

The Association of Theological Schools in the United States and Canada. *2024–2025 Annual Data Tables*. Pittsburgh, PA: ATS, 2025. https://www.ats.edu/files/galleries/2024-2025_annual_data_tables.pdf.

Research contributing to the development of the Pastoral Training Model was supported in part by initiatives funded by the Lilly Endowment Inc.

SELECTED WORKS BY MICHAEL A. MILTON RELATED TO PASTORAL FORMATION

Milton, Michael A. *Ancient Wisdom, Living Faith*. Eugene, OR: Wipf and Stock Publishers, 2026.

Milton, Michael A. *Finding a Vision for Your Church*. 2nd ed. Eugene, OR: Wipf and Stock Publishers.

Milton, Michael A. *The Pastoral Decision-Making Model*. Charlotte, NC: Bethesda Publishing Group, 2023.

ADDITIONAL WORKS BY MICHAEL A. MILTON ON PASTORAL MINISTRY

Milton, Michael A. *A Seminary Professor's Plea for Scholarship in the Church*. Tryon, NC: Bethesda Publishing Group, 2023.

Milton, Michael A. *Called.*

Milton, Michael A. *Deep Roots (Christian Vocation in Context: The D. James Kennedy Institute of Reformed Leadership)*. Eugene, OR: Wipf and Stock Publishers, 2025.

Milton, Michael A. *Hit by Friendly Fire: What to Do When Other Believers Hurt You.* 2nd ed. Eugene, OR: Wipf and Stock Publishers, 2025.

Milton, Michael A. *Involved with Mankind: A Theology of the Chaplain Ministry*. Tryon, NC: Bethesda Publishing Group, 2023.

Milton, Michael A. *Leaving a Career to Follow a Call.* Eugene, OR: Wipf and Stock Publishers, 2000.

Milton, Michael A. *Lost and Found: Public Theology in the Secular Age*. Eugene, OR: Wipf and Stock Publishers, 2024.

Milton, Michael A. *Silent No More: A Biblical Call for the Church to Speak to State and Culture*. Dallas, TX: Fortress Books, 2013.

Milton, Michael A. *So, What Are You Doing Here? The Role of the Minister of the Gospel in Hospital Visitation*. GRIN Verlag, 2018.

Milton, Michael A. *The Sacred Roll Call.*

Milton, Michael A. *The Secret Life of the Pastor (and Other Intimate Letters on Ministry)*. Fearn, Ross-shire, UK: Christian Focus Publications, 2015.

Milton, Michael A. *Walking the Tightrope.*

Milton, Michael A. *What God Starts, God Completes.* 4th ed.

ACKNOWLEDGMENTS

There are many people to thank for their support of this significant project. It is significant not only because of its subject matter, but because it represents four years of concentrated research, coursework, writing, and editing undertaken in the midst of an active life of ministry.

As always, I am deeply grateful for the steadfast encouragement and wise counsel of my wife, Mae. Her quiet strength and constant support made this work possible. My son, John Michael Milton, also contributed thoughtful insight and practical encouragement in the development of the project.

I am especially indebted to my longtime colleague and friend, Dr. R. J. Gore. At the time of this project's development, Dr. Gore served as Dean of the seminary and Professor of Systematic Theology. His scholarly wisdom, encouragement, and collegial partnership strengthened both the proposal and the vision behind this work. Though I had previously completed a PhD in theology at the University of Wales (1993–1998), years of pastoral ministry confirmed for me the need for further research into sustainable pastoral formation. Together, we prepared the grant proposal to the Lilly Endowment, whose generous support made this project possible. I am deeply grateful to the Lilly Endowment for recognizing the importance of strengthening pastoral ministry for the good of the Church.

I also wish to recognize Dr. Rebecca Rine, Senior Fellow of the D. James Kennedy Institute of Reformed Leadership, whose editorial skill and academic insight greatly enriched the work. It was a distinct privilege to have her guidance and assistance in the management of the grant and the refinement of the manuscript. During much of this period, my assistant was Mrs. Christine Hartung, whose faithful administrative support helped sustain the progress of this project. I am grateful for her diligence and encouragement along the way.

I also express sincere appreciation to the Board of Trustees and advisors of Faith for Living, Inc., whose encouragement and commitment to the mission of the D. James Kennedy Institute of Reformed Leadership have helped sustain this work. I am grateful for the wisdom and support of Dr. George Grant, Mr. Jeff Johnson, Mr. Kent Warner, and Dr. R. J. Gore, together with the valued counsel of our advisors, Mr. Steve Maye and Mr. John Michael Milton. Their shared commitment to strengthening pastors and congregations has contributed meaningfully to the vision embodied in this project.

Finally, I offer sincere thanks to the many students, pastors, and ministry leaders whose experiences, questions, and faithful service helped shape the vision reflected in these pages.

With gratitude to all who have contributed, I humbly commend this work to Almighty God, praying that He would be pleased to use it for the strengthening of His shepherds, the building up of His Church, and the advancement of the Gospel of Jesus Christ in this world; through the same Jesus Christ our Lord, to whom be glory in the Church and in all generations, world without end. Amen.

ABOUT THE D. JAMES KENNEDY INSTITUTE OF REFORMED LEADERSHIP

The **D. James Kennedy Institute of Reformed Leadership**, a ministry of Faith for Living, Inc., a North Carolina 501(c)(3) Nonprofit Corporation, exists to equip Christian leaders for faithful service in the Church, academy, and public square.

Named in honor of the late Dr. D. James Kennedy—pastor, theologian, and founder of Coral Ridge Presbyterian Church—the Institute continues his legacy of Gospel proclamation, theological education, and cultural engagement.

The Institute provides:

- pastoral leadership training
- research and publications
- ministry development programs

The Shepherd's Path Pastoral Residency represents the Institute's flagship effort to strengthen pastoral formation for the Church in the twenty-first century.

Seminary professors, students, denominational leaders, church judicatories, pastors, and congregations may learn more about courses related to the Pastoral Training Model by visiting https://djkinstitute.learnworlds.com/

Learn more about the course in pastoral residency: https://djkinstitute.learnworlds.com/about

---

ABOUT MICHAEL A. MILTON, PHD

Michael A. Milton
PhD, DMin, MDiv, MPA

Michael A. Milton is a Presbyterian minister, educator, author, and public theologian whose work integrates pastoral ministry, theological scholarship, and cultural engagement in service to the Church and the Great Commission. He serves as President and Senior Fellow of the D. James Kennedy Institute of Reformed Leadership and is the founder of Faith for Living, Inc., a North Carolina 501(c)(3) nonprofit corporation devoted to Christian discipleship, leadership development, publishing, and cultural engagement.

Dr. Milton previously served as Chancellor and Chief Executive Officer of Reformed Theological Seminary and currently serves as Distinguished Professor of Missions and Evangelism at Erskine Theological Seminary. His academic work reflects a commitment to renewing pastoral formation by integrating theological education and mentored ministry. His research on pastoral resilience, vocation, and ministerial sustainability contributed to the development of the *Pastoral Training Model* and the *Shepherd's Path Residency*.

He holds a Master of Public Administration from the University of North Carolina at Chapel Hill, a Doctor of Philosophy in theology, a Doctor of Ministry in higher education leadership, and a Master of Divinity degree. He conducted postdoctoral research in Higher Education Teaching and Learning and earned a certification in

Higher Ed Teaching from the Bok Center at Harvard University. His interdisciplinary training reflects a lifelong commitment to scholarship in service to the Church.

Dr. Milton is also a retired United States Army Chaplain (Colonel), having served more than three decades in military ministry, including service in the United States Army Reserve. His chaplaincy experience has informed his theological reflection on vocation, pastoral care, leadership, and public theology.

He is the author of numerous books addressing pastoral ministry, theological formation, public theology, Christian vocation, and the relationship between faith and culture. His work emphasizes integrating intellectual rigor, spiritual formation, and practical ministry to strengthen pastors and congregations.

Through Faith for Living, the D. James Kennedy Institute, and related ministries, Dr. Milton continues to contribute to the preparation of Christian leaders who proclaim the Gospel of Jesus Christ and serve faithfully in church, academy, and society.

To receive resources on Christian discipleship, leadership, and public theology, subscribe to the Faith for Living newsletter:

michaelamilton.com

Learn more about the writing ministry of Dr. Milton here:

drmilton.live/books

www.ingramcontent.com/pod-product-compliance
Lightning Source LLC
LaVergne TN
LVHW050642100826
845148LV00011B/1954

* 9 7 9 8 3 8 5 2 6 9 5 3 2 *